THE MOON LOOKS DOWN

KENNETH McALL

BORN IN CHINA in 1910, Dr. Kenneth McAll graduated in medicine from Edinburgh University. On his return to China in 1937 his experiences there led to interest in the powers of possession and he has devoted his life since to the curing of psychiatric illness through divine guidance. His unique book on this subject HEALING THE FAMILY TREE (Sheldon Press) has become an international bestseller.

He has practised as a Consultant Psychiatrist in England for twenty-five years and is an Associate Member of the Royal College of Psychiatrists.

FRANCES McALL

DR FRANCES McALL graduated in medicine from Edinburgh in 1939. She has worked in general practice at the same time helping Kenneth to run their home as a small nursing home for his patients and bringing up their five children.

She has served on the National Executive Committee of the Medical Women's Federation and the Country Executive Committee of the Women's Institutes. She is also a member of the 'Federation of Doctors Who Respect Human Life'. She is the author of FOR GOD'S SAKE, DOCTOR! (Grosvenor Books).

Frances & Kenneth,

FRONTISPIECE: 'Instead of the barbed wire shall come up the morning glory.'

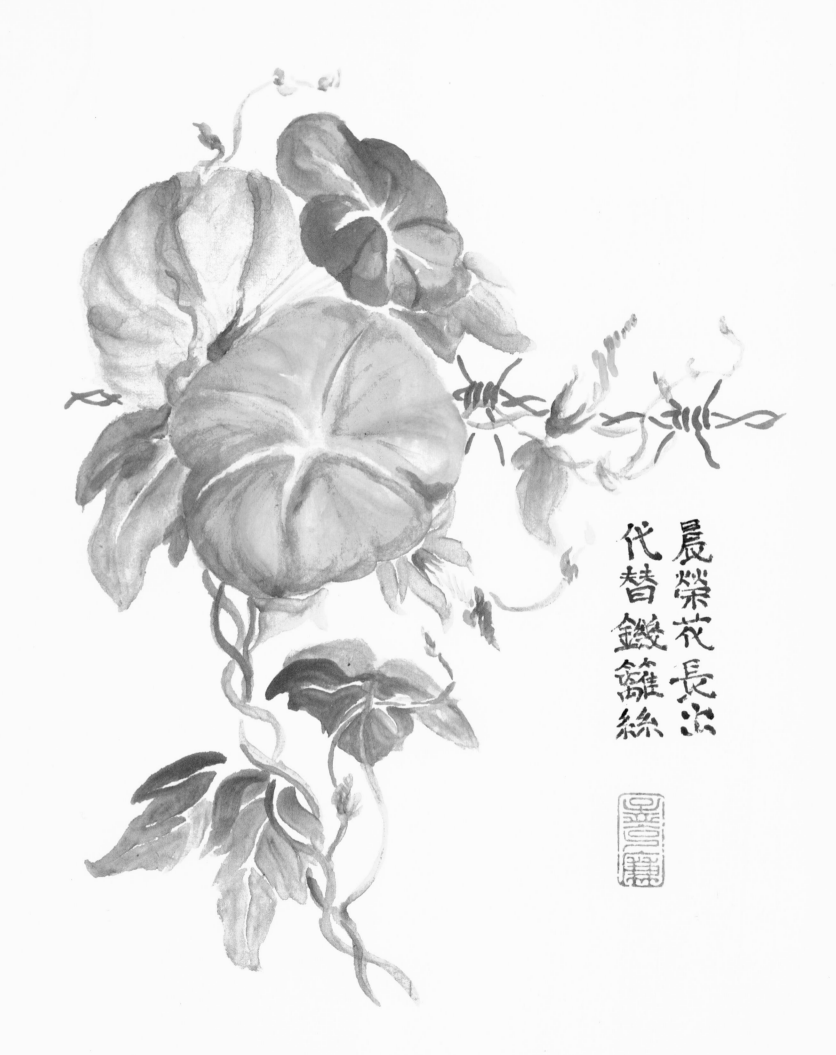

晨榮花長次
代替鐵籬絲

THE MOON LOOKS DOWN

月
光
之
下

FRANCES

AND

KENNETH McALL

DARLEY ANDERSON · LONDON

First published in Great Britain in 1987
by Darley Anderson, Estelle House, 11 Eustace Road, London sw6 1JB.

ISBN 1 869833 05 X

Designed by Bob Wright.

Typeset, printed and bound in Great Britain by William Clowes Limited, Beccles and London

EVERY STORY must needs be told from the story-teller's point of view so some degree of one-sidedness is inevitable. Only certain memories endure through time and each person has his or her own. These happen to be ours and we realise that some of our friends, reading this book, may feel that important details have been left out or presented in an unfamiliar light. We hope they will understand and we would like to acknowledge our own debt of gratitude to all who contributed through self-sacrifice, effort and prayer to the unexpected richness of this war-time experience. As the book will reveal, we ourselves owe more than we can say to Godfrey and Betty Gale who, with Margie, stuck by us and put up with us throughout, providing us with a solid basis of faith, fun and friendship. Betty kept a diary and on this I have been privileged to draw for events which I had forgotten or overlooked.

To all surviving fellow internees we send our warmest greetings.

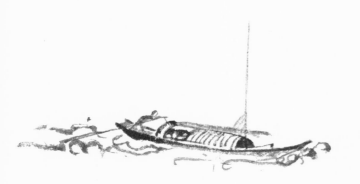

When you turn to the right hand or when you turn to the left,
you shall hear a voice behind you saying,
'This is the way. Walk you in it.'

Isaiah 30.21.

月光之下

CHAPTER 1

FOR THE FIRST of many times my heart beat so loudly I felt sure it must be audible to everyone else particularly the grim-faced Japanese soldier who was deciding whether or not to let us off the station without a minute search of us and our possessions.

Ken held up an impressive pass issued to him two years earlier by an official in Peking and now well out of date but a cunning placing of his fingers over the original date hid this fact from the soldier who was duly impressed and waved us through.

If he had examined us more carefully he would have found wads of sweaty illegal bank notes strapped round our waists under our clothes. Japan at that time was in firm day-time control of the Chinese railways and the towns that lay along them in all but the extreme west of the country but in the countryside it was a different story. Here the Communist eighth route army, known simply as the 'Ba Lu' to the locals, was master and it was only their printed money which was acceptable in the villages. Anyone using the official Japanese currency was in for serious trouble. The Chinese money had to be obtained secretly in Tientsin and smuggled through the Japanese lines.

Ken, with one and a half years' experience behind him, was quite used to all this. China, anyway, was familiar ground to him. He had spent his first nine years in Hankow where his parents were missionaries who had their own fill of adventures. He had arrived back as a missionary himself in the autumn of 1937, the year of the Japanese invasion of China, along with Godfrey Gale, an old friend from school days. Because of the war which had closed all Chinese ports to foreign shipping, they were taken to Japan where the local authorities put them up in a cold, bleak hostel in Kobe. From here they managed to do some sight-seeing, conscious always that they were being followed, before being offered space ten days later on a troopship crowded with Japanese soldiers for a stormy crossing to Taku, the port for Tientsin in north China.

Then followed the Mission's statutory and enjoyable spell of six months in the Peking language school before Godfrey went south to join the staff of a large University hospital in Tsinan while Ken, after a few months training in another Mission station where he spent some time skating up and down the Grand Canal, had been sent to Siaochang where he was now in charge of the eighty-bedded hospital.

Siaochang was a small village typical of the hundreds dotted over the immense north China plain. It was forty miles from the railway and the road to it was no more than constantly changing cart ruts across fields of millet growing to a height of six or seven feet in the summer or bare frozen ground in winter. The countryside was almost annually inundated by floods from the Yellow river to the south so most villages were built on slightly raised ground and each one kept at least one boat.

Now, since the invasion by the Japanese two years before, the area was the constant setting for battles, skirmishes and ambushes between the wandering Japanese army trying desperately to get control and the guerillas of the Ba Lu. This had not stopped the age-old business of banditry from flourishing on the side as well, so every journey was fraught with hazards and delays. The only transport, apart from bicycle, was by mule cart and it was more comfortable and almost as quick to walk.

The Mission cart was in Techow to meet us, driven by a jovial character, Dan Sen who had seen service with the Chinese labour force in France during the first world war and who was inordinately proud of his one English sentence—'Give us a kiss, dearie', which he trotted out on any appropriate or otherwise occasion. To my surprise, though not to Ken's apparently, I saw dozens of Chinese piling their belongings on to our cart though they all had carts of their own. The reason became clear when we crossed the wooden bridge over the Grand Canal, guarded at each end by more Japanese soldiers. All the Chinese carts were thoroughly searched but ours was graciously exempt. As soon as we were over the bridge and out of sight, the excess baggage on our cart was duly reclaimed by its various owners. Dan Sen doubtless benefited from this service.

The countryside looked peaceful enough for the journey to our first home together. I had arrived in China after a journey from England which had taken , thanks to the outbreak of world war two in September 1939, an unexpected four months. It had included being delayed in India for six weeks, being blown up by a mine outside Singapore and narrowly surviving a typhoon in the South China seas. I had already learned something of what it is like to be scared

BRIDGE OVER GRAND CANAL

月光之下

and also something of what it means to know that God is real and always available under any circumstances. I was to know a lot more fear in the years to follow but never to lose that certainty. Six months at the language school in Peking had been a gentle introduction to China and getting used to the Japanese presence. On a brilliant June day we had been married. There had been thirteen nationalities represented at the wedding—Americans, Germans, Japanese and Chinese as well as British, a glimmer of hope for the future perhaps.

Now it seemed the most natural thing in the world to be tramping with Ken across the seemingly endless, dusty plain of North China as we had tramped together over the Pentland hills outside Edinburgh when we were both medical students. But the natural suddenly turned into something else when I felt a hard object poked into the middle of my back. I glanced sideways at Ken and saw out of the corner of my eye the nozzle of a rifle sticking into the middle of his. A voice in Chinese barked an order which, with only six months knowledge of the language behind me, meant little to me. 'Don't look round', Ken said, as though this was quite a normal event.

The rifle held by an unknown hand, prodded us gently, as long as we kept moving, towards a large gate. Once through the gate it was firmly shut behind us. We found ourselves in a courtyard jammed with carts and people and animals. After a few moments we were ushered into a room on the right where, seated at a table were three uniformed officers. The middle one politely asked us who we were, where we were going and what did we do? After we had told him we worked in the Mission hospital he wanted to know what we hoped to achieve. We told him we believed that the only hope for the world was a change in human nature and that only God could bring this about. 'A very good idea', he commented with a smile, 'but too slow. Our way is much quicker.' With that we were dismissed and after waiting for two hours, everyone was suddenly allowed to go. We could only assume that there had been some military action in the area which they would prefer us not to know about.

Once again we were thankful not to have had our baggage searched. We had spent our honeymoon in Japan with a family we had known well in Britain and hidden in the middle of the cart was a bundle of Japanese New Testaments wrapped up in a tell-tale Japanese cloth which they had given us to pass on to any Japanese soldiers we might have a chance to get to know. Such a find would hardly have gone down very well with our Chinese Communist captors.

We spent the night in an inn where we fed on a large bowl of noodles topped off with a poached egg and slept on tables to avoid the animal and insect life which abounded on the floor. Somehow I slept quite well.

After a breakfast of noodles we set off again, slightly ahead of other early morning travellers. All seemed to be peaceful until I noticed a lone figure standing on a slight rise on the side of the road a little way ahead. 'A bandit', remarked Ken, 'pretend you haven't seen him.' This was easier said than done. I found it particularly difficult to keep my eyes from not looking at the ominous bulge concealed in his loose jacket. However he took no notice of us either and we passed by without a word being said. A hundred yards or so further on we dared to look round. All the other carts had been stopped. Bandits were not always so lenient towards missionaries. Possibly this one felt he might one day have need of our help so had better not molest us.

CHAPTER 2

THE MISSION STATION with its church, school and hospital had been in Siaochang for seventy-five years. The hospital was the only one practising western medicine and surgery in an area as large as Wales with a population of ten million people. Its eighty beds were always full and out-patient clinics consisted of a stream of people queueing past a table at which the doctor sat issuing instructions to the extremely capable head nurse.

During his year and a half there, Ken had averaged two and a half major operations a day, often tackling surgical problems unknown in this country and of the sort which would be left to a senior Consultant to handle. But Ken's natural flair for surgery, he was top of his class as a student, saw him through and the patients as well. In addition to operating he would see several hundreds of out-patients and was on call for maternity emergencies. He was the one who had to supervise building alterations and hospital records, accounts, laboratory and dispensary. Because of the war and bandit situation in the countryside, he had to take days off to travel to Tientsin to purchase and bring back essential drugs and equipment. Fortunately he had a very able and experienced Scottish Matron and quite remarkable young nurses whom she had trained.

There had previously been a Chinese doctor as well but it was now considered too dangerous for him to stay. The Ba Lu were only too ready to pick up anyone who might be of use to them or to imprison anyone who did not agree with them. All Christians were at risk. As it was, the Communists were among the greatest users of the hospital, bringing in a steady stream of wounded or sick soldiers, men and women. The hospital policy was to accept anyone needing help and no one was asked too closely about what they had been up to. We realised that it was almost certainly the usefulness of the hospital which kept the Mission there. We heard later that, as soon as we and the Japanese had departed, all the Mission buildings including the hospital were pulled down as though to wipe out the very memory of us.

At the same time that we were useful to the Communists, we were a nuisance to the Japanese. They felt we helped to keep up an anti-Japanese morale in the area and probably

月光之下

suspected us of spying. Because of this they felt obliged to maintain a presence in the village and to do this they had built a small mudbrick walled fort just outside the village and close to our compound wall. Out of this they would stream by day to harrass the countryside trying to seek out the Ba Lu and if necessary burn villages in which they were suspected of hiding or receiving assistance. It was a common sight to see a plume of smoke where a village had once been. At night they retreated back into their fort and it was then the Ba Lu got busy. It was the local farmers who suffered most. By day they were made to construct roads for the Japanese transport or put up telephone wires and by night they were dragged from their beds to dig up the roads and pull down the wires.

The Mission compound stood in a very vulnerable position between the Japanese fort and open country. The Ba Lu would frequently use it as a shelter from which to launch their mortar attacks on the Japanese who, of course, would then open fire in their direction. We became quite used to shells flying over our heads. The hospital itself was situated a few hundred yards from the compound nearer the village and to reach it meant crossing an open space in full view of the Japanese. Any shadow spotted moving after dark was fired on without warning which made it very much a No Man's land at night. For safety's sake Ken would quite often sleep in a small room in the hospital near the entrance.

It was during one of these nights several months before I joined him that he was woken in the small hours by the pressure of a hard object on the side of his head. A voice from the dark told him to keep still and not call out. It then demanded that a certain patient be handed over. Ken refused, adding that he did not know the names or occupation of his patients. Finally the voice said that he and his friends would find the patient themselves and, leaving one of their number still holding the gun to Ken's head, they slipped silently out of the room. Shortly after, somewhere outside the hospital, Ken heard a burst of gunfire and found himself alone once more in the dark. Sure enough, in the morning, a body was discovered lying on a hospital blanket outside the building. It was that of a patient who had broken both legs and both arms after jumping down a well in an effort to escape being caught by the Communists. He was almost certainly a Japanese spy.

The question now was how would the Japanese react to the incident? The possible repercussions were alarming. At this time, Eric Liddell, the famous Olympic runner, had come to Siaochang to help with the evangelistic work. As this side of Mission work was not appreciated by either the Japanese or the Communists, Eric was given the title of hospital business manager and in fact, did help Ken with this side of his work as well as doing his own and shared a house with Ken. Early in the morning they sat down together and asked God to tell them what they should do. They both felt that Ken should go by himself as soon as possible to see the Japanese Commander who, up to that time none of the foreigners had met, and tell him what had happened before anyone else could do so.

Just as the sun was rising and with a white hospital coat on so as to be conspicuous, Ken approached the fort with some trepidation, very uncertain of his reception. The event could well have strengthened the Japanese belief that we aided and abetted the Chinese army and they tended to be anything but gentle when angry, alarmed or made to look foolish.

It was some time before Ken could make the guards at the gate of the fort understand that he wanted to see their 'Number one.' Eventually, after much gesticulating all round, he was taken to the Commandant's office which was full of soldiers. Ken suspected from the atmosphere, that the night's happenings were already known. The Commander himself was lying on his bed and, without turning to look at Ken, he barked, presumably at him, in the way only an angry Japanese can bark. He then ordered everyone except Ken to leave the room. This was all done in Japanese with appropriate signs. When they were alone he rolled over, sat up in bed, grinned broadly and in faultless American, invited Ken to sit down saying as he did so 'Forget it, Buddy.'

He had already heard what had happened and after discussing the affair, he went on to tell Ken that he had grown up in California and that his mother was a Christian. He hated the whole business of war especially the killing which, as a soldier, he was forced to do, and longed to be free of it all. After a long talk about these things, Ken left feeling he had made a good friend out of his feared enemy.

Shortly after this the garrison was changed and a fresh lot took over but on a day in the following December when, after a separation of two years Ken and I had just met, we were standing on the quayside at Tientsin waiting for my trunks and hand luggage which had just been unloaded from the river steamer to be checked by the Customs officials. A voice behind us said, 'Dr. McAll, what are you doing here?' and, dressed in the uniform of a Customs officer and with a broad smile on his face was the ex-Siaochang commander. Seizing a piece of chalk from one of his subordinates, he scrawled a large white cross on all my belongings which remained unopen instead of, as was usual at such times, being opened, rummaged through and more than likely turned upside down on the pavement.

He was clearly unwilling to say too much in front of his colleagues but asked us to meet him at a certain café that evening after dark. It was my first evening with the Mission and our going out straight away was not too popular but we felt we could not disappoint him. When we arrived at the café he was already there, now in civilian clothes and, sitting round a small table in the dimly lit room he told us how, soon after his talk with Ken he had been offered this post as senior Customs officer, a job for which with his knowledge of English, he was eminently suited and was very much enjoying.

月光之下

CHAPTER 3

ONE OF THE CASUALTIES of the fighting around Siaochang was a man who had been brought in with his head partially severed from his body. A message was brought to the hospital by villagers who had found him after a group of Eighth Route army soldiers had been ambushed by the Japanese. All the others had been successfully executed and their bodies had fallen into the grave which they had been made to dig themselves. They had taken this survivor and hidden him behind an idol in the local temple. Eric Liddell and a nurse went out to the village to fetch him and somehow he survived the rough mule-cart journey back to the hospital.

Ken carried out a successful repair job but the best surgery could not avoid the tell-tale scar which extended from his right ear round to the left cheek. It was some time before he could speak at all. When he did it was to call Ken to his bedside in perfect English and to tell him that he was a graduate of the Peking College of Fine Arts. He had been on his way home when he had been pressganged into service with the Ba Lu. Being a staunch pacifist he had refused to carry weapons whereupon they had made him do their secretarial work. When they were ambushed and lined up for execution he was at the end of the line and refused to kneel. Being a tall man, the much shorter Japanese soldier whose arm must have been tired by that time, was unable to do a clean job but in spite of this the wounded man who had fallen into his self-dug grave had been left for dead.

He went on to say that he had been watching Ken and the nurses as they worked and this had impressed him deeply. Could Ken please tell him more about this Jesus he had heard talked about? He refused to divulge his true name promising to do so when he felt it was safe but with the new faith he now found, he called himself 'Lee Shin Sheng'—Lee 'Heart Born.'

His one great fear was of being recognised either by the Communists or by the Japanese and there was no way in which he could hide the ugly scar on his neck and face which he felt might give him away. The question was what to do with him when the time came for him to leave hospital? After talking it over with Eric, Ken suggested he should be taken after dark to a neighbouring village where a Christian family would be willing to hide him until he was fully recovered and hopefully forgotten in the Siaochang area. He was then to return to Siaochang and make straight for our house in the Mission compound where he could stay as long as necessary.

Ken put aside a room for Lee's use and this he turned into a studio where he produced exquisite paintings of flowers and birds and gave Ken lessons in Chinese painting. After I joined the household, he took on the job of teaching me Chinese and proved a most gentle and patient teacher. If any Chinese or Japanese soldier came near the house he would bolt into the kitchen and put on an apron supplied by our redoubtable cook, Chou Shih Fu.

The few months I spent in Siaochang after our marriage were lonely ones. Everyone else had their work to do and Ken was seldom at home. Even when he was he would be on call or busy with hospital work. Because of my lack of language I could do little to help apart from giving the occasional anaesthetic or attending the baby clinic to learn what I could from Matron who ran it. My main souce of entertainment came from an unexpected quarter.

One morning about 11 a.m. I heard the heavy clumping of boots outside the house and through the front door marched about ten Japanese soldiers. They dumped their rifles just inside the door, came into the sitting room and sat down. At first I felt mildy alarmed but they were all smiles and clearly ready to enjoy home comforts. I asked Chou Shih Fu to produce tea and biscuits. As usual when he was doubtful about anything, the corners of his mouth turned down and he grunted disapprovingly. However he did it, though to hand round refreshments to Japanese soldiers must have irked him very much. Having done it he then retired behind the screen put by the door leading to the kitchen to keep out the draught. The Japanese could not see him but I was well aware of his comforting presence.

Once I had recovered from the initial shock of the invasion, my maternal instincts surfaced. They were a pathetic group of boys in much-worn uniform and down at heel boots. The only smart one was their young officer. None of them spoke English but, as well as the New Testaments, the Mitsuis had also equipped us with tourist guides and maps of Japan exactly right for this sort of occasion. As the soldiers pored over them they excitedly pointed out to me where they lived. Japanese soldiers never had any home leave and they suffered from home-sickness as much as any of us. I was pretty home-sick myself at that time.

Having drunk their tea and eaten most of our biscuits they then produced out of their tunic breast-pockets small books of national songs which they usually sang while marching. The officer had a very pleasant tenor voice and with me at the piano trying to make something out of the tonic sol fa and put some harmony to it, we worked through the book. One particularly haunting song, 'The moon looks down over the deserted city' was to follow us right through the years of the war. At night in the internment camp we would hear the sentry on duty humming it below our window. When I visited Japan a few years ago it was the first music played over the intercom as we landed at Tokyo airport.

This mid-morning visitation became quite a regular feature of my day and I almost looked forward to it as my one small contribution to peace on earth. Chou Shih Fu was always at his post behind the screen and Lee remained out of sight in the kitchen. On one occasion I found a rifle left behind in the hall and had to run after the retreating soldiers to give it back to its owner, the only time any of us was likely to handle a Japanese gun.

The fact that soldiers could walk into our homes without any warning made us feel very vulnerable. Three of the unmarried ladies shared a house in the far corner of the compound.

月
光
之
下

Annie, the hospital matron, was ill in bed one day when a Japanese soldier much the worse for drink, marched into the house. One of Annie's friends who happened to be at home, watched helplessly as the soldier, pushing her to one side, proceeded to stump up the stairs in his dirty boots. Halfway up was a full-length mirror. The soldier stopped abruptly, clapped to attention, saluted smartly, turned round and marched unsteadily downstairs and out of the house.

CHAPTER 4

OUR DEPENDENCE on a wisdom beyond our own often became a matter of life and death under wartime conditions. Perhaps if we only knew it, it always is. Ken and Eric and the other Chinese mission workers too, frequently had a sense of being directed as they travelled round the area.

One day Ken was returning to Siaochang along the rough road through the fields and heading towards a village when he was aware of someone behind him who told him not to go to that village but to go instead to another one away off to the right where he was needed. Ken took it to be a local farmer who knew what was going on. When he reached the village the gate was opened and he was pulled inside. The villagers asked him what had made him turn out of his way so Ken said 'That man out there told me to come,' but when he and the other men looked out there was no one about. Then Ken realised that the voice had spoken to him in English—unlikely for a Chinese farmer. The villagers then told him that if he had continued the way he was heading he would have landed in a Japanese tank trap and that the village he was making for was occupied by Japanese troops. There had been a local skirmish which had left several wounded who had been brought into the village.

Amongst these was a man who had heard Ken talking about his work on one of the occasions when Ken had been picked up for questioning by the Eighth route army. The man had been so interested he wanted to hear more and thought the only way he could do this was to get himself wounded and taken to the hospital. Having failed to get himself wounded by someone else he had shot himself through the thigh fracturing his femur. When night came Ken had him carried to the hospital while he himself stayed behind to do what he could for the other wounded men. While in hospital the man decided to become a Christian and his leg healed well. However he still insisted on limping and using crutches, finally admitting to Ken that this was the only way he could avoid being forced back into the Communist army. The Mission offered to put him through a teacher's training and he later joined the staff of the college in Tientsin in which Eric Liddell had taught.

The Mission school in Siaochang could only accommodate primary school children. For the next stage they had to go to Techow, the town on the railway. Travelling at any time was fraught with difficulties but the constant fighting in the area added to the natural hazards of flooding had made it almost impossible. There were twenty children needing to be taken to Techow and three times parents had set out with them only to be turned back by rumours of bandits or fighting. Ken, still fairly new to the situation at that time but needing to get to Techow himself to pick up supplies, offered to escort them.

Early in the morning the children were rounded up from the nearby villages and the procession set off with a cart and several wheelbarrows carrying their baggage. It was slow going. Four times flood water had to be crossed, Ken and the children being punted across in flat-bottomed boats while the cart struggled through with water up to its axles. It was dark by the time they reached the village where they were to spend the night. It was so dark in fact that Ken could not find his way to the inn. Because of fighting in the surrounding district during the day, everywhere was tightly shut up, only one old man still around who offered them the hospitality of his pig styes. Ken bedded the children down in the straw and lay himself across the entrance.

As they still had a long way to go and as no one carried watches for fear of getting them stolen, Ken decided that they should start off again when the first cock crowed. It was still very dark when he was suddenly awakened by the unmistakable sound of a cock crowing. Having shaken the unwilling children awake, he got them on the move again. They stumbled along in the darkness expecting every moment to catch the first glimpse of the rising sun but no sun rose. Every now and again a wheelbarrow would tip over into a muddy ditch, the cart having been abandoned long before when the water had been too deep for it. Finally the dawn broke just as they were approaching another village where they learned they had been walking for four hours. Ken admitted he must have been mistaken about the cock and was duly apologetic.

The rest of the journey was uneventful apart from more water over which Ken had to ferry the children one at a time on his back, and they arrived safely at their destination. Three days later he returned by the same route but when he arrived at the village in which they had spent the night, he found it burned down and completely deserted apart from two old women scrummaging around in the rubble for anything that might be worth salvaging. They told him that just after he and the children had left that morning, the village had been raided by Japanese troops who apparently expected it to be full of the Eighth Route army guerillas they had been chasing all the previous day. They had taken away all the carts, men and boys before setting the village alight. Everyone else had fled.

All this had taken place long before any self-respecting cock would be thinking of crowing.

月光之下

CHAPTER 5

IN SIAOCHANG I was learning, as Ken had been over the previous year, to see the war from both sides. One night we were visited by a charming Eighth Route army officer who told us amongst other things that he had been trained in Moscow some years earlier for the eventual takeover of China. The army's orders were to harrass the Japanese as much as they could with minimal loss of men and weapons leaving the serious fighting to the Nationalist troops further south.

The morning after his visit, the equally charming, newly-appointed commander of the Japanese garrison also dropped in for a chat. He too spoke fluent English with an American accent and confided in us that he had been posted to Siaochang with instructions to force us to leave, so relieving them of an unnecessary presence in the area. As we were not enemy aliens at that time but merely undesirable ones, he had to devise ways and means of making life intolerable for us and our Chinese colleagues. He greatly regretted having to do this he told us. On this particular morning he was in a particularly confiding mood. He had just found his newly made roads dug up once again by order of the very man who had been with us the night before. 'Gee! What do you do with these guys?' he had asked as he threw himself into one of our comfortable armchairs. We offered our sympathy but no more.

It very soon became clear that he was attempting to carry out his instructions to force us out of the area. An early effort on his part was to organise an anti-British demonstration outside our compound wall. A stage was built from which speeches could be made but a convenient wind blew this down. The villagers, apart from one or two whose way of life clashed rather obviously with that taught by the Mission for over half a century, were our friends. Having been ordered out to join in a march protesting at our continued presence, they were obliged to obey but on reaching the compound they dispersed back to their homes leaving the Japanese without an audience.

Then came pressure on the actual running of the Mission. Increasing restrictions were placed on the movements of Mission personnel. The Chinese Communists helped in our demise by opening up schools of their own which local children were forced to attend. In the hospital the Japanese insisted that all admissions, operations and discharges should be notified to them daily. At first this was to be done in English but later they asked for the lists in Chinese and Japanese as well. As there were no Japanese speakers among us this was difficult. There were threats to the Chinese nurses if they continued to work for us.

As the pressure increased it became clear that for the sake of our Chinese friends and colleagues we would have to move out. We saw it as no more than a temporary move and expected to be back before long. So on a bitterly cold January day carts were loaded with our personal possessions, space being left for us to sit on whenever we chose to ride rather than walk.

Travelling in our convoy for their own protection were our servants and Lee. He had promised that when we reached the railway he would tell us his real name. Apart from the cold which caused icicles to form between our noses and the top of the rug in which we were huddled, the journey proceeded without any hold-ups. By this time I was nearly three months pregnant and with the ruts in the fields frozen into rock-hard lumps, I felt safer trudging along on my feet, only riding on the cart when my feet became too numb.

We thought of the comfortable home we had left and the solid old-fashioned furniture which Ken had so lovingly and skilfully modernised before I arrived. We thought of the wedding presents we had had to abandon. I had already lost all those given to me before I left England when the ship was sunk in Singapore harbour. I can still feel pangs of sorrow over my camera, a 'thousand flower' pattern dinner service and the biscuit barrel with its eight Chinese immortals serenely circling it.

At the railway we parted company with our Chinese friends. They were to spend the night in the local inn before taking the train to their various destinations. We were bound for the American Mission which often gave us hospitality on our journeys. We had planned to meet up again with Lee and the others at the station in the morning but when we arrived there was no sign of them so we never did know Lee's real name though we still treasure some of his paintings.

Our next stop was to be Tsinan, the ancient capital of Shantung province. Ken and I had been invited to join the staff of Cheeloo University to work as medical officers to the students, employees and teaching staff until such time as we could return to Siaochang. For us it was quite an emotional experience as Ken's father had worked in the University for thirty-three years up to his retirement translating medical textbooks into Chinese. His office had not been used since he left and the desk drawers still contained some of his belongings.

The University occupied a large area just to the south of the city and outside the city walls. Beyond it were the mountains. Inside the city walls were several staff houses and a very fine modern hospital equal in standard and in some ways ahead of anything we had known in Britain. The whole outfit was run jointly by American and British missionary societies with a mixed Chinese and foreign staff who lived in houses scattered round the campus. The students were housed in dormitory buildings in a remote area of the campus. Ken and I in our capacity of medical officers were the only foreigners allowed into them. This was a privilege we exploited to the full.

We were given a small house to live in furnished with the basic necessities and a small garden in which, amongst other plants, was a beautiful pomegranate bush. Next door to us lived the Gales. Godfrey was now the Ear, Nose and Throat surgeon in the University hospital. He

月光之下

had married Betty, a Canadian nurse, whose father was teaching in the University and who herself had grown up in China. She too was pregnant at that time and our dates almost coincided exactly. She was older than I and much more experienced in the art of housekeeping. Her support over the next few months was something I could hardly have done without, though she actually had a way of supporting everyone within range. We were to get to know each other better than any of us suspected in those early days.

I was going to need someone to take on the cooking and the marketing but before we could even feel concerned as to who this should be, Chou Shih Fu, knowing we could not possibly manage without him, turned up on the doorstep and took us once more under his fatherly wing. I knew little enough about cooking, shopping or running a home even in English but Chou Shih Fu invariably treated me as though I, rather than he, was the expert. Each morning he waited on me for my instructions and I would wrack my brain trying to think of something to eat and then attempt to translate it into Chinese. I am sure he did not need the translation but he pretended he did. My suggestions were usually met with the turning down of the corners of his mouth and a polite 'T'ai kuei'—'Too expensive.' Then having gone through the motions of respect, he would go off and do what he thought best.

CHAPTER 6

LIFE SETTLED DOWN into the daily routine of morning clinics, with Ken seeing the men and I the women. The ones who helped me most with my Chinese were, of course, the ones who could not speak a word of English. Very soon I was able to ask them where the pain was or whether their bowels were functioning normally. The educated ones always wanted to practise their English so were less helpful. Ken spent much of his time in the hospital and to my surprise even I found a niche there. The hospital had just installed its first electrocardiogram but there was no one who understood it. A non-medical member of staff had read up what he could but without medical background it was not easy to interpret the results. As the most recent graduate from medical school I was the only one to have met the ECG so was promptly put in charge of it. This gave me a great sense of importance which had been lacking up to that time as I had felt particularly useless.

We delighted in getting to know the students, all of them hand-picked from their various schools. We would have long discussions with them in their dormitories, Ken with the boys and I with the girls and several of them took to invading our home in their free time. They were all products of Mission schools. Government education, apart from the old traditional teaching of the Chinese classics, was still in its infancy so many were already at least nominally Christians. We passed on what we ourselves had learned when we were students about the possibility of listening to God as well as talking to Him and so finding out what He wanted done. A few began to meet regularly with us to do this. It seemed a very natural development to at least one of the girls whose father was a Buddhist. From her childhood she had remembered his getting up at 4 a.m. each morning to meditate for two hours.

All this was a refreshing change from the endless round of hospital work in Siaochang and it seemed to make much more sense to be training young Chinese who would all be likely to move into responsible positions, to do the job themselves. We could happily have spent our whole lives in such a set-up but history intruded and forced us into a rather different path.

By now the war in Europe was well under way. The Chinese in the occupied areas of China were unable to voice their opposition to the Japanese but it was clear that amongst thousands of the foreigners in the country anti-Japanese feeling was mounting. We listened daily to a news broadcast put out by an American broadcaster sponsored by Maxwell House coffee whose verbal offensive against Japan forced him to have to wear a bullet-proof vest and we often wondered just what was his life expectancy.

As the summer approached he became more and more belligerently anti-Japanese. We had by this time, become quite used to passing the armed Japanese guards at the city gate whenever we went to the hospital or shops but we sensed a growing tension in the air. This was crystallised for us when word came that a ship would be available for any women and children who wished to leave and we were warned that there might not be another opportunity. It was as though the day had suddenly gone dark. Ken did not press me one way or the other but left it to me to decide. Humanly speaking with all the uncertainty about what might lie ahead and with our baby due in July, it made sense to go, but into my mind came a picture of an unknown length of time separated from Ken with the added difficulties after the differing experiences we might go through, of our ever getting close together again. We both had felt very strongly that it was God who had told us in the first place to get married and I could hardly imagine He would want us to separate again at this early stage. I felt I should stay and that we should face whatever the future might hold together.

Betty, after packing and unpacking, reached the same decision and we decided then to stick together as far as possible for the mutal support we were going to need and for the sake of the babies we were both expecting. There was only one occasion in the next four years when I was going to doubt our choice.

As the weather became hotter and hotter Betty and I got heavier and heavier. Ken and I slept on bamboo matting on our netted verandah sweating it out. One night I felt a tickle on my neck. Half asleep I brushed my hand across the tickle only to wake with a start realising I had brushed off something much larger than a mosquito. Ken switched on his torch and there lying on my pillow was a large scorpion.

月光之下

As July approached, Chou Shih Fu became more and more motherly. Each day at 11 a.m. he would make me sit down to a bowl of rice gruel and stand over me while I consumed it. In the middle of July Betty disappeared into hospital and produced a daughter, Margaret. The next ten days seemed more like a year to me as the temperature soared into the hundreds. Finally the English gynaecologist decided I had had enough and took me in. That day the hospital staff went on strike.

Once away from the countryside we had almost ceased to be aware of Communist activity only to be reminded of it when one of our student friends told us that until she had decided to become a Christian, she had been secretary of the University Communist Party. Such a party would certainly have been banned if anyone had known of its existence. Now on July 27th the hospital nurses were told that unless they stopped work their names would go on a black list to be remembered when the Communists eventually came to power. A handful of nurses belonging to a very strict and often despised Christian group calling themselves 'The Little Flock' refused to strike. Every now and then during that long night, in spite of all the other work they were carrying, one of them would put her head round my door, cheerful and comforting as I went through an uncomfortable first stage of labour feeling sick and alone. She showed no signs of the fact that she and about seven others were coping with the whole hospital and facing a very threatening future. I have often wondered what happened to them during the cultural revolution.

Ken and the other doctors stayed in the hospital all night too, doing what they could. He was on duty in the out-patient department the next morning when Elizabeth finally decided to arrive, her thumb going straight into her mouth where it retreated frequently over the next few years. The day she was born the rains came, the grass turned green and the temperature fell. It was also the day on which the Japanese froze all American and British assets in the country.

CHAPTER 7

HAVING A BABY alters one's whole perception of life as well as its pattern. It is one thing to trust one's own life to God and quite another to do the same with one's child. I often thought of the security of my English home forgetting that already children in Britain were being separated from their parents in order to find some safe hiding place for them.

It was a great help having Betty in the next house but her baby, Margie, was a placid person who did all she was supposed to do and steadily gained weight. Elizabeth cried a lot, seemed to dislike feeding, bringing back most of what I did manage to force in and consequently failing to put on weight. My stupid reluctance to admit that, in spite of being a doctor, I did not know how to manage a new baby, cost a great deal of unnecessary anxiety and a few tears. Finally, when she was three months old, I pocketed my pride and approached our excellent American Paediatrician who without hesitation, having examined Elizabeth and found nothing basically wrong, recommended mashed potato. From that moment she never looked back, nor did her fondness for potatoes.

It was none too soon as in September a further evacuation took place and this time several of our more senior colleagues took the opportunity to get out. Among them was Dr. Scott, the Paediatrician. Before she went she presented Betty and me with a small bottle of highly concentrated vitamin oil one for each baby. We were grateful then but were to be even more grateful by the end of the war.

Now there was a baby to play with the students tended to visit us even more, and several of them became close friends. One day one of them suggested that we might work out a plan for their morning quiet times which they had all begun to practice. This could then be printed on a card as something they could keep when they left the university. One Saturday morning in December we were together in our sitting room when we all felt a sudden sense of urgency about getting this card printed at once and that we should do enough to distribute widely round the students. There seemed no special reason for any rush but three of the students went to the University press only to find that as it was Saturday the press was closed. However as one of the boys knew how to use the machine they were given permission to do it themselves. They worked until after midnight producing several hundred cards printed in Chinese on one side and in English on the other. The next day, Sunday, they distributed them round the University keeping a few for their own families and friends outside.

Monday was a special day as for the first time a Chinese student, one of our friends, was taking the morning assembly in the chapel. I was playing the organ. Ken was not there as he had to do an early clinic in the hospital. Godfrey had also gone to work. The service went well and I had just finished playing when one of the foreign staff came hurrying over to me and whispered 'The Japanese have attacked Pearl Harbour. You'd better get back to your house as quickly as possible.'

I did move quickly. Back in the house I had left Elizabeth in the care of a sixteen year old Chinese girl, Shih Ying, and I certainly did not want the Japanese arriving there before me. This was the day we had been fearing and we had no idea how the Japanese would react. All of us had experienced something of their rough handling. If we had omitted to bow to the sentry at the city gate we risked being hit with the butt of his rifle. I had once had a suitcase opened and turned upside down on a muddy road and had to collect my belongings while a young soldier made passes at me with his bayonet. We had seen their own civilians suffering similar treatment at the hands of soldiers on a train. We had become familiar with stories of their atrocities in the countryside. But it was with a strange sense of detachment that I ran back to

月光之下

our house wondering whether, now that they had us in their power, they would just come in and bayonet the lot of us.

My first action after sending a frightened Shih Ying back to her mother, was to find a luggage label and on it to write Elizabeth's name and the home addresses of Ken's and my parents. I remembered a story of an English baby girl found by villagers after her parents had been executed by the Communists. Because of a label tied to her clothing she was finally restored to her grandparents in England. I then hunted down a rucksack and packed it with as many essentials for a baby as I could. Having done this, I sat down and waited to see what would happen. Out of the window I saw the first Japanese soldier in the campus. Chou Shih Fu must have been out shopping and there was no sign of Betty at that moment.

Nothing happened. Betty was the first to turn up. She had been down at the hospital early that morning examining student nurses and had arrived at the city gate just as a lorry was unloading dozens of soldiers all armed to the teeth, who proceeded to march across the road and into the University campus. This was the first she knew of anything having happened. In a panic she rushed after the soldiers, and, joining the Japanese army for a few hectic moments, she was swept through the University gates which clanged shut behind her. In the general excitement and confusion no one noticed her and when the army was ordered to turn left she turned right and kept running till she reached home.

Immediately the news of Pearl Harbour came through, the hospital was closed and guards put on all the gates. No one could get in or out, but Ken, an explorer by nature, discovered a tortuous passage in the basement through which ran all the heating and water pipes. He followed the pipes and found himself in an empty part of the building with an unguarded door. He arrived back at the campus just ahead of the army. The rest of the medical staff were held in the hospital until the afternoon when, much to everyone's relief, they were allowed home.

CHAPTER 8

THE JAPANESE soldiers took up their positions round the campus perimeter in a completely orderly and disciplined manner. In place of the thought that we might all be bayonetted dawned the realisation that we might be in their hands for a very long time. One or two of our student friends had managed to sneak up to our house so say good-bye but by the end of the day every Chinese was off the premises. One of the girls who had heard of the rush to get the Quiet Time card printed wanted to know how we knew that war would break out that day!

The first action of the Japanese was to close all the University buildings putting seals on the doors. The hospital too was closed and no new patients were to be admitted. As soon as those patients now being treated were well enough they were to leave. Our servants were given the choice of leaving at once or remaining shut in with us. Chou Shih Fu who, to my immense relief had returned safely from the market, never considered leaving at that point. The Gale's servant, known affectionately as Red Jewel departed very unwillingly under pressure from Godfrey and Betty, only to return a few days later happy to make himself a voluntary prisoner. He proved to be more than a Jewel to us.

As the Chinese servants were forbidden to leave the campus at any time, Chou Shih Fu now had to instruct me in the art of shopping. As the Japanese had no way as yet of feeding us, we had to be allowed to look after ourselves and buy our own food. On the first day those needing to go shopping were ordered to meet at the University gatehouse where an escort would be provided to take us into the city. We all felt rather like large and ungainly barges as a small Japanese soldier with a rifle over his shoulder emerged to take us in tow. Having walked in front of us through the city gate he then decided it would be wiser to keep an eye on us from behind and drive us with the occasional bark like a flock of ewes. On reaching the shopping area we all wanted to go different ways leaving our escort utterly confused in the middle of the road surrounded by local inhabitants who clearly thought it very funny indeed. The Chinese have a somewhat twisted sense of humour not unlike our own. Rather than risk further loss of face, we were allowed from then on to go shopping on our own as long as we reported to the guard on duty at the gate, a process which often entailed endless hanging around. It did, however give us the chance to slip in a quick visit to friends inside the city wall and on one of these occasions we met up with two of our student friends who were full of an idea for organising our escape. They planned to kidnap Ken, Elizabeth and myself and smuggle us out through the Univesity perimeter fence under cover of darkness. We would then move towards free China travelling by night and hiding in a village by day. Many students were already planning to get out and make their way to the west and eventually large numbers of them did and continued their studies. But it was a bit different for a foreign family travelling with a small baby to care for and I was timidity incarnate.

Spring came and went and we were once again sleeping out on our verandah. Night after night I would wake up with a jerk wondering if this was to be the night. No one else as far as we knew, had any idea of what was in our minds. Then one day we heard it was all called off. The father of one of the scheming students was a secret agent of Chiang Kai Shek's who regularly visited the north incognito to spy on both the Communists and the Japanese. His opinion was that although there should be little difficulty in eluding the Japanese, the journey would involve getting us through about five hundred miles of Communist held territory over which his Nationalist friends had no control. If they caught us they would almost certainly hold on to us and force us to work for them. He strongly advised against the attempt. Ken and the students were disappointed that it had all come to nothing but I slept well for the first time that night.

月光之下

CHAPTER 9

THERE WERE PLENTY of other things to keep us on our toes during the first months of partial internment. The supervising of the closing down of the hospital was put into the hands of a Japanese corporal who in civilian life had been a backstreet shop owner, or so we heard. It certainly soon became clear to us that he was a first-rate bully with scant knowledge of matters academic or scientific. One of his first acts was to tear down and destroy the apparatus for a valuable soil research project which was on the verge of success and to break up the University printing press, scattering its type to the four winds. One of the Chinese doctors found the costly electrocardiograph machine on the local street market and bought it back for a song.

Every day for about a fortnight, Rufus the hospital business manager would be sent for by 'Bill' as we called him. Foreign accounting methods was something else he knew nothing about and whenever he felt particularly muddled he would knock Rufus down, kick him and put lighted matches up his nose. Or he would make him kneel while he carried out a mock execution with his large sword. Rufus was an ex-professional footballer who could have sent the little corporal flying with one blow from his fist. In fact he said he had to lie on his hands and 'pray for the grace of God' to prevent himself from hitting out. Day after day he would come home bruised and shaken but never once did he complain or retaliate. However word somehow got out to the local Japanese community about Bill's behaviour. They courageously complained to the military authorities who respected their complaint and the little corporal was sent back to the front and a more senior and competent officer put in his place.

When we saw what was happening to valuable property, we or rather Ken, decided to try and smuggle anything we could out of the campus and into the city where our Chinese colleagues could pick it up. This meant breaking into various buildings and houses vacated by staff and then getting the 'loot' out. To break in often meant breaking windows after dark and forcing locks on doors. Books, porcelains, equipment and paintings were taken out. Some were packed into a box and pushed out through the fence where someone was ready to collect it. Other things had to be taken past the guards at the gate. Ever since I first met Ken, I have found it almost impossible not to do something he has expected me to do. Whether it was climbing enormous beech trees in Scotland, going out in a fragile bamboo canoe of his own making in rough seas or trudging along muddy tracks in the dark waiting to be shot at, I had to do it. Now Betty was involved as well. We were expected to push the two babies in their prams and out through the gate knowing that underneath each child were valuable scientific instruments. The Japanese are famous for their love of children and we exploited this to the full, but the grins on

25

our faces as the soldiers tickled the small girls under their chins were entirely artificial and once again our hearts pounded away, it seemed to us, both visibly and audibly.

This time we got away with it but on another day the guards' suspicions must have been aroused. Instead of playing with the children and waving us through, they ordered us to lift the children out of their prams and our secret was uncovered. 'Take those things to the Commandant!' one shouted and we sheepishly turned the prams round and started off in the right direction but fortunately we were soon hidden from the gate by the high hedges and having reached this point we made a dash for home the children greatly enjoying the race. That was enough for us and we insisted that if the men wanted to get any more out they must do it themselves.

But we were not allowed to give up quite so easily. In April the Japanese ordered us to leave our own houses and join up with others in a larger building occupied at that time by two men on their own. Ken satisfying his usual curiosity was exploring the cellar of this house and found that what appeared to be a wall of more recent origin had been built across the middle of it.

He knocked out a brick, put his hand through the hole and felt a crate on the other side. This he managed to prise open and lifted out a small earthenware bowl. On the University staff was an Englishman, a Baptist missionary, who was considered to be one of the greatest experts on Chinese culture. Ken took the bowl to him for identification. When Mr. Drake saw it, he flushed deeply and turning his back on it said, 'Don't tell me where you found it.' He told Ken he had uncovered the findings of a Canadian expedition, removed from Anyang the ancient capital of China. The excavations had been done with the permission of the Chinese government some years previously but permission had not been given to remove the treasures from China. Then the Japanese had invaded so the leader of the expedition had hidden them as best he could before returning to Canada.

Ken felt that if he could find them so easily so could the Japanese and they would not hesitate to carry them all off to Japan. He therefore decided to re-hide the whole collection. This proved to be larger than expected and mainly consisted of heavy bronzes as well as pots and oracle bones which the ancient kings used for divination. Nothing daunted, Ken started to prepare various sites for burial. Seals had been put over the doors of our original homes but he found he could get into ours through a cellar window. He moved the pile of coal stored there and took up the brick floor digging a large hole underneath it. This took several weeks to complete by night and candle light and each time my heart was somewhere near my mouth until he arrived back safely.

One day while he was working in the cellar, he heard heavy footsteps approaching the house. The front door was opened and he held his breath as the owner of the feet began to tramp through the house. At that point he climbed out of the window abandoning his spade and made for home. When he returned a few days later, he found boot marks in the dust leading up to the door of the cellar where they had stopped and turned back. His digging was undisturbed.

月光之下

Late one evening after dark, the prams were laden with treasures, so laden in fact that they could not move without squeaking painfully, more than enough to alert any passing sentry. Betty and I followed the men who were carrying all they could in their arms and after a short distance, the squeaking became so ominous that we were obliged to abandon the prams and do likewise. We had to go down paths between hedges and in my imagination behind every hedge and shrub lurked a sentry waiting to pounce. But the objects were successfully buried, the cellar hole filled in, bricks replaced and the coal shovelled back on top. Some other things were buried in a hole under the body of a dog which had been found conveniently dead on the premises.

CHAPTER 10

AFTER A WHILE our money supplies began to dwindle and we were forced to think in terms of producing more of our own food. We were not lacking in experts in any field and agriculture had been an important part of the University's curriculum. The man in charge, another Canadian in whose house we were now living, organised us all into work shifts and got us out on the campus digging. We not only had to dig for planting but for irrigation as well and the campus was criss crossed with trenches which could be opened up or closed according to where the water was needed. It was hard work but gave us something constructive to do.

'Red Jewel' had stayed on with the Gales and was now doing the cooking for all of us. Chou Shih Fu had left some time before. His old mother had turned up one day having covered a hundred miles or more on her bound feet. She brought a request from her village that he should return to head up the local guerilla group there, and she refused to budge until he agreed to go. It was a sad moment for us.

The University had as part of its agricultural programme, a herd of goats. The idea had been to improve the local stock by crossing them with American breeds. The Gales had taken over one of these goats, Shasta by name, who had provided milk for Margie and Elizabeth from the time they needed more than Betty or I could give them. The Japanese Commandant turned out to be a goat enthusiast who recognised the value of these animals and decided to have them confiscated and shipped to Japan.

We were duly alarmed at the thought of losing our milk supply and were even more alarmed when, one night, Shasta disappeared. However the next day and every day for the next six months, goat's milk appeared on the table. Red Jewel had pushed Shasta out through a hole in the fence where a friend had taken her and each night at midnight milk was delivered through the fence without the Japanese ever finding out.

Meanwhile the Japanese had turned the University into a military training camp. They occupied all the main buildings and lectures were given in the church which stood in the centre of the campus. We often watched as soldiers were made to run round the grounds, fully equipped, in the heat of the summer. If one should falter, he was made to stand with his arms above his head while an officer beat him with his rifle butt.

Towards the end of the summer, rumours began to circulate that all of us were to be repatriated. By now there were about seventy of us left. The British government we gathered, was sending a ship to bring back people likely to be useful to the war effort in exchange for Japanese civilians. On their list were doctors, nurses and teachers and most missionaries fell into one or other of these categories. Sure enough, early in August we heard that all our names were on the list and we were to leave for Shanghai within a few days. The Japanese told us we might sell our belongings and we were to have the saleable goods outside our homes on the following morning. It sounded a good idea and we certainly needed the money.

For Ken and me there was little to do as we had already abandoned our household goods in Siaochang but for many, Cheeloo had been home for a great number of years, and early next morning outside each house was a pile of furniture, kitchen equipment, bedding and the rest. We had been told to price everthing so labels were stuck on with what we considered to be appropriate figures.

The first to come round were the Japanese military who promptly slashed all the prices by half. Then the University gates were opened and in flooded the local populace, Chinese and Japanese to descend like vultures on our possessions. We stood by helpless and watched as those who happened to want the same article bargained for it in time-honoured style using the 'stone, scissors, paper' method.

The Japanese graciously allowed us to hold on to basic furniture until the next day but this was almost impossible. Three times Red Jewel chased after prospective buyers who had taken our dining room table and as we ate, unknown Chinese stood over us ready to snatch away our plates as we finished with them. At one point when Godfrey stood up to get something, his chair was whisked away and he had to finish his meal standing up. After all this the Japanese took all the money which had been paid over. With the prospect of going home none of this seemed to matter. In fact we took it all as a huge joke.

Then came our own packing. We were all reduced now to personal belongings and any bedding we might have kept. We had given several blankets to a Swedish couple in Tsinan thinking we would not be needing them again. As Ken painted our name on our boxes, he was tempted by the large space of the now pictureless wall of the sitting room. With a great flourish, in Chinese style, he painted a picture of bamboos tossing in the wind and rain and in Chinese characters which the Japanese also use, he wrote 'The wind blows and the rain falls but the love

月
光
之
下

of God has made you strong.' After the war visitors to the house which had been occupied by Japanese after we left, told us that the painting was still there.

On a roasting hot August afternoon we set off. No rickshaws were allowed into the campus so we had to carry our own things as far as the gate. Outside was a fleet of rickshaws all ready to fight for our custom and after the usual hard bargaining we piled in. All the way to the station people waved as we passed and on the platform itself were many old friends, staff and students to see us off. The Japanese took little notice and seemed only too happy to be getting us off their hands. For us it was a mixture of sadness at having to leave and excitement about actually being on our way home.

CHAPTER 11

THE TRAIN was already packed with foreigners from further north. The coach reserved for our party had been shut up all day and the temperature in the four berth compartment which we were sharing with the Gales, was 108°F. We were told we might open the windows but that as soon as darkness came the blinds must be pulled down in case guerillas saw the lights and decided to shoot at the train. We would have preferred to take a chance.

The journey was to take two days and we had to provide our own food. As well as food we carried milk for the children but in that heat it was sour almost before we started. Eighteen-months-old children seem perpetually thirsty and it is hard to explain to that age why they couldn't have a drink when they wanted one. Fortunately they managed to settle down quite quickly on their makeshift beds on top of luggage on the floor and slept through the night.

We were thankful that they did. In the early hours of the morning we heard confused sounds outside in the corridor and discovered that our friends, two couples in the compartment next to ours, had been taken violently ill with diarrhoea and vomiting. As the morning went on they became steadily worse until they were having to be carried to the toilet, no easy matter on a swaying train along a narrow corridor. At one point they all looked as though they could not take much more and we were seriously worried. Cholera is endemic in China and naturally this was what we feared and there was no way in which adequate fluids could be got into them. Godfrey and Ken did their best to help while Betty and I kept ourselves firmly shut in with the small girls.

It was not only we who feared cholera. At the first station of the day, our coach was disconnected and shunted into a siding where we sat sweating it out, trying to keep the babies

29

amused and praying for our friends. To everyone's relief the journeys along the corridor became fewer and when eventually a Japanese doctor arrived he pronounced us free of cholera and was content to spray us all with disinfectant before leaving. It transpired that the four victims had brought meat sandwiches with them for which the heat had proved too much.

The railway came to a stop when it reached the great Yangtse river, at this point two to three miles wide. We were decanted from the train and on to a ferry which, by the time we were all on board, had sunk to within a few inches of the water level. The water was quite rough as well as fast flowing and as small waves constantly splashed over the gunwales we seriously doubted whether we would ever reach the other side. It would certainly not be the first or the last Yangtse river ferry to capsize in midstream. After what seemed an eternity the south bank got steadily nearer and once arrived we were once more loaded on to a train for the last few hours' journey to Shanghai.

It was late at night before we finally emptied out on to Shanghai station almost too exhausted to stand. As there were no seats to sit on we settled for the filthy floor while we waited for something to be done about us. In the small hours of the morning we were put on to buses and taken to the outskirts of the city where the Japanese had commandeered the Columbia Country Club now deserted by its former American users. Many people, most of them missionaries from central China, had already arrived and a group of them had volunteered to wait up for us. One of them I recognised as an old family friend and collapsed almost unconscious into her arms while someone else removed Elizabeth from mine. We were given as much as we could drink and bundled into camp beds in rooms already partially occupied by others. This I only discovered when I came to the next day. Elizabeth and I were sharing a room with a young mother and her two children. Her husband was a business man and therefore not on the list of 'wanted' by the British government but their names had been put on because of his wife's severe asthma. Betty and Margie were in a room nearby with another family. The men found themselves allotted to the bowling alley with ninety-eight other men and boys. Those who could not be accommodated there were sleeping in the bar.

Having recovered from the first of several nightmare journeys we were ready once more to feel excited by the prospect of getting away. My main memory of my reactions on the third morning we were there is of total disbelief. We had been informed that each of our names was on the ship's list but when a list appeared on the notice board I only recognised three names out of the three hundred now waiting in the club. We questioned and argued but no other list was forthcoming and no changes made. It was only later we heard that as many people as possible in Shanghai had climbed on to the Embassy band-wagon, signing on as secretaries, under-secretaries, nannies and under-nannies to embassy staff who were legitimately top of the government list. Who could blame them? With them went most of the doctors who had served the British community in Shanghai.

It seems extraordinary to me now looking back, how quickly the three hundred of us in the Country Club (built to sleep 35), settled down to the situation and accepted the fact that we

月光之下

would be in Japanese hands now for the duration. The ship we did not go on was lovingly re-named the 'Swindle Maru'. As time went on we realised that we were probably as a group, far better equipped to stay behind than many of those who had gone. Teachers, nurses, doctors would all be urgently needed in the days to come.

There were casualties on the altered list. The young mother later died through lack of available treatment as did a fine young diabetic who died when supplies of insulin ran out.

CHAPTER 12

THE NEXT few months were a strange mixture of freedom and captivity. We were allowed to go out and about in Shanghai provided we wore red armbands with which we were issued. These had on them a 'B' for British or an 'A' for American plus a personal number. The three of us were 'B184, 185 and 186' respectively. There was also a book near the front door which had to be signed every time we went in or out. There were several homes open to us in the area and we made good use of them. Visiting Chinese friends needed care as it did them no good to be seen fraternising with us. However some of them joined us in secretly visiting British friends in their flat where we could talk and pray together. We would be careful to arrive separately and leave at different times and this added a certain spice of adventure to our meetings.

Life in the club itself was anything but comfortable. A bowling alley does not make an ideal dormitory as the camp beds provided by the Japanese were not wide enough to span the gully, which meant sleeping with the bed at an angle. There was no room to walk as everyone's belongings were stacked round the beds. Those in the bar were not much better off. Unattached women had to sleep with their beds along the walls of the upstairs corridor with no privacy. Apart from the crying of other people's children at night and worse still, one's own, plus the endless smell of dirty nappies, we were better off than most. All of this would not have mattered for two or three days but the days lengthened into months and winter came. Whatever you do with a camp bed it is impossible to get enough warmth underneath and Shanghai nights can be very cold. Meals were taken around the now disused swimming pool which was a favourite spot for all Shanghai's flies to get together. We fed the children with one hand while the other kept the flies on the move. The food itself was of quite good quality.

During the time I had been held up in India on my way out, I had picked up amoebic dysentery. This continued to haunt me for the next few years. It attacked while we were in Shanghai and I was taken into the very fine China Inland Mission hospital for treatment. While I was away Ken had to look after Elizabeth. This would not have been too difficult if it had not

31

been for the fact that no men were officially allowed upstairs and it was certainly impossible for him to have Elizabeth with him in the bowling alley. He often had to attend to her needs after the other family in our room had gone to bed so had to feel his way in the dark. Having located Elizabeth he then had to determine whether or not she needed changing. She invariably did and it is not an easy matter even for a more experienced mother to change a nappy by feel only. The memory of this has remained with him.

The Japanese now had to set about finding long-term accommodation for the 8000 or so enemy aliens now in their hands in the Shanghai area. We had grown almost accustomed to our pseudo-liberty until one day, without any warning, the Japanese descended on hundreds of British and American men, some in their homes and others picked up by lorries off the streets. It was not entirely indiscriminate, many of those taken being men holding some public position. They were all put into a large building in the middle of the city where we learned, they were to be held as hostages for Japanese civilians held in allied countries.

The friends whose flat we frequented, were at home with their two small children when two Japanese officers arrived. He was told to pack a small bag immediately and was about to be taken away when they discovered they had got the wrong man. They were looking for a Major in the Salvation Army who happened to live on the floor above. Our friends left them to make this discovery for themselves which sadly they did leaving his sick wife and two teenage children to fend for themselves. However there were many who were apparently picked up at random and for a few days no one knew who would be next.

A few weeks later more unattached men, 1200 of them, were rounded up and taken off to the first of the regular internment camps named by the Japanese 'Civilian Assembly Centres'. This was in an area across the river from the main city where most of the buildings were factories or warehouses. The building in which the men were put had been a tobacco factory later used as a warehouse and finally condemned even for this purpose. It bordered on a village which had been reduced to rubble by the Japanese invasion in 1937. We could only imagine what it might be like and hoped for better things for ourselves.

It was March before our turn came and we were told to prepare for a move. We were to equip oursleves somehow with beds and food utensils. Most people went out and bought the cheapest type of things which one might take camping, tin bowls and mugs and iron bedsteads. There would be no chance to replace breakables but in any case none of us envisaged it lasting very long and there was no point in being extravagant. We did not even know whether or not husbands and wives would be kept together so had to prepare for separation which seemed a real possibility.

In spite of this uncertainty Ken and I had the strong feeling, which we both felt came from God Himself, that we should spend what remained of our money on a really comfortable upholstered day-bed which would serve as a double bed at night and a settee by day. It was an act of faith which paid off handsomely as most do.

月光之下

Betty went into a Japanese shop in the city to buy warm nighties for Margie. She wanted a size that would last her a long time but when she got back to the club she found she had been given ones which were too small. She hurried back to the shop to change them only to be met by a stony refusal to even look for any others. In spite of Betty's pleadings, telling him that with internment ahead they might not be able to buy anything else for years he still responded with an unsmiling 'No'. Betty then became desperate and almost in tears began to shout rudely at him before storming out of the shop. Outside she wept with rage and frustration but by the time she arrived back at the Club she was feeling ashamed of her behaviour and the fact that she had lost her temper. As she went to sleep that night she thought of all the hatred in the world and how she had only added to it.

When morning came she headed back for the shop. It took her twenty minutes to screw up her courage to go in. The Japanese shopkeeper looked surprised to see her and even more surprised as she gulped out an apology for her rudeness the previous day. It was like the sun coming out as a smile came over his face. Having thought him extremely ugly the day before he now looked almost beautiful. They shook hands over piles of children's underwear and wished each other well. Sadly he could find no larger size of nightie but Betty left the shop feeling she was walking on air.

CHAPTER 13

A COMMITTEE was set up to work out with the Japanese authorities who should go where. Two other camps were to be opened in Shanghai itself using school and University buildings and three were to be up-country in the ancient city of Yangchow where three mission compounds had been taken over. Each camp would need medical cover and each would hold three or four hundred people. The Gales and us still hoping to keep together, allowed ourselves to be allotted to 'B' camp in Yangchow.

The morning of March 8th 1943 was bitterly cold as we gathered at 8 a.m. in the grounds of Shanghai Cathedral, a fitting starting off point. Each of us had been issued with a luggage label on which was written our camp and number. We were allowed to take a trunk each and as much hand baggage as we could carry. The trunks along with our beds had been sent on ahead. Godfrey and Ken had made slings for carrying the children on their backs. Ken had found some tough blue cloth and parachute webbing to do this with. This left both hands free for carrying bags and cases of varying descriptions. Betty and I had all the usual clobber which

33

has to accompany young children including toys to keep them amused on the journey. We had no idea how long this would take or even how we would be travelling.

Here in the Cathedral courtyard we were able to take our first look at our fellow internees. Of course several were friends who had been with us in the Club and for us it was a relief to be away from the discomfort there. We were already partially processed for prison life. The rest could hardly have looked more desolate and forlorn. Most of them up to that moment had been able to continue living in their luxurious, centrally-heated apartments and very few looked the sort who might ever have enjoyed camping conditions or experienced any form of deprivation. We wondered whether some of the women had ever carried anything heavier than a fan. We could not help feeling very sorry for them.

At last the order to move was given and we set off in a long crocodile on the first of several similar long trudges, this time through the Shanghai streets to the famous Bund by the river. Presumably it was meant to be a humiliating experience for us but with the streets lined with people many of whom smiled and waved, we felt more like heroes—but heroes going where was the question.

An impressive looking boat was moored out in the river and we were taken out to it in sampans and once on board were rather forcibly shown our accommodation. The men were taken off to a whole deck of crude bunks—it was a troop carrier, while Betty and I were shown to cabins. Betty and Margie were put in a cabin with two elderly ladies and Elizabeth and I in another with two more ladies. As we had put all the children's things together it seemed more sensible to be in the same cabin rather than running backwards and forwards between the two. Little did we realise how such action would be frowned on. Our fellow passengers were only too pleased to change places so Betty and Margie moved in with Elizabeth and me. It all seemed very innocent and all went well until a Japanese officer came round to take a roll-call. His fury at our presumption knew no bounds and for the first time Betty and I were really scared. We were ordered not to leave our cabin for any reason until given permission to do so. We felt like two little girls being punished by the headmaster and punishing it was. It was very stuffy in the cabin and as the morning wore on we all became very hungry and thirsty having had an unusually early breakfast. It became increasingly difficult to keep the children's minds off the need to fill their tummies and relieve their thirst. Not only this but our bodily requirements became more and more urgent. In desperation we tried the door only to find it locked and no amount of knocking made any impression. We were indeed prisoners.

About 2 p.m. we were ordered out and escorted to the dining saloon. A delicious smell of curry greeted our noses. It seemed that everyone else had already eaten as the saloon was empty. We felt even more like naughty girls. When the meal was put in front of us it consisted of very small bowls of rice covered with curry so hot that when I took a mouthful I felt I was losing the entire mucous membrane lining my mouth. I saw Betty go red and open her mouth to gulp in cool air. My heart plummetted. If things were going to continue like this however were we going

月光之下

to keep Margie and Elizabeth properly fed? There was no special provision for two year old children. We did our best to dig out the unsullied rice from the bottom of the bowls and managed to get a few meagre mouthfuls into each of them.

We trailed back to our cabin to be locked in again feeling almost as hungry as we had been before and with two still unsatisfied complaining infants.

Godfrey and Ken had been forbidden to visit us but later in the afternoon, they boldly approached the Commandant of our new camp who was travelling with us and he graciously granted us a reprieve.

We arrived the next morning in Chekiang on the Yangtse river in pouring rain and were decanted first on to the quayside and then into flat-bottomed barges for the trip up the Grand Canal. Once again Ken and Godfrey loaded their daughters on to their backs as we picked up our luggage. Soldiers were posted on either side of the gangplanks down which we had to go and we were counted like a flock of sheep. There was no deck as such to the barge but Betty and I found a slightly sheltered spot under a plank where we settled down on the hard dirty floor with the children.

Very soon we heard the sounds with which we were to become so familiar of Japanese soldiers barking their distrust and disapproval. The rumour spread that two prisoners had escaped. There was much stamping around and more shouting until someone had the bright idea of suggesting that they might have missed counting the two small girls on their fathers' backs.

In the ordinary way we would have felt it a great privilege to be journeying by barge up the famous Grand Canal. It was built in 300 B.C. to provide a means of carrying rice up to the Emperor's court in Peking. The rice was demanded as tribute from the southern provinces. Built along the Canal at intervals were fortified cities to guard the Imperial route. Yangchow was one of these and probably the most famous and beautiful. The Emperor Kublai Khan being a foreigner himself, preferred to employ foreigners to govern the cities and Marco Polo had held this position in Yangchow for many years in the 12th century.

Betty and I, apart from the occasional glimpses of the top of tall junk sails as they passed by, were only aware of our aching arms as we held two sleeping infants and the extreme hardness of the bottom of the barge. The relief of arriving at Yangchow several hours later and passing through the magnificent Marco Polo gate to the city was short-lived. A few rickshaws were hailed by the Japanese and the most elderly in our party were ushered into them. The Commandant also rode. The rest of us were lined up, laden once again with all we could carry and the children on their fathers' backs, this time carefully counted by our ever-counting guards.

They must have chosen the most roundabout way to go and the walk became more and more like a marathon, or felt like one. Ken and Godfrey were, of course, carrying the heavier load and there was nothing Betty or I could do to relieve them. We felt increasingly our new prisoner status as the guards roughly kept us moving along but just as we began to feel we could not manage another step, the small cavalcade of rickshaws overtook us. In the leading one was the Commandant who, with a smile, invited Ken to dump the luggage he was carring in with him. A lady travelling behind him took in Godfrey's load and our hearts rose again.

Our destination was an abandoned American Mission school and in the relief of arriving, we hardly noticed the high brick walls and the large wooden gate which slammed shut behind us.

CHAPTER 14

IT ALL SEEMED pleasant enough with the Spring just beginning to show itself. One of our lasting memories of this camp is of the beautiful weeping willow tree on which a golden oriole frequently sat and held forth in glorious song quite oblivious of the chaos being created by the foolish humans sharing the world with him. It was also the tree round which a young priest would walk saying his daily offices. He would start punctually at 11.55 a.m. and finish at 12.05 p.m. thus completing matins and evensong at one go.

There was the main school building in which classrooms had been turned into dormitories and two or three smaller two-storeyed staff houses. It was in one of these that the Gales and we were to share a room which was of reasonable size with a small cupboard adjoining it. The outlook over the garden was quite pleasant but we were not high enough up to see over the compound wall obviously built to keep out undesirables and now eminently suitable for keeping us in.

All the rooms were bare of course, so our only furniture was our beds and trunks which had arrived ahead of us. The Gales were surprised to find their trunks strangely light, but this was soon explained when on opening them Betty found that nearly all her winter clothes had gone, some of Godfrey's woollen underwear was missing as was a new doll which had been given to Margie by a friend in Shanghai. There was great sorrow over this. Betty wondered who was wearing the first new outfit she had bought in three years and wished she had let Margie pull out the doll's eyes when she had wanted to. Ken and I were more fortunate but many other people found things missing and some belongings replaced by bricks to make up the weight. We never knew of course who had taken them but realised what a temptation they would be to the hands through which our luggage had to pass and just hoped they would be put to good use.

Settling in produced difficulties we had not thought of. We had all grown up in respectable homes in a respectable age and the problems of who should undress first was a real one. We had arranged the children's home-made cots halfway down the room thus providing a

月
光
之
下

modest screen between them and us. Even so it took courage to start but that was the only night on which we felt any embarrassment. Three years later we never gave it a thought.

The next morning we were summoned to roll-call on a grassy patch presumably used by the school as a playing field. The three hundred and fifty of us were lined up in rows while two or three guards fussed around us like sheepdogs. Once again there was consternation when the counting showed two short. The trouble this time was that they were in fact too short, Margie's and Elizabeth's heads barely reaching halfway up the guards' ceremonial swords. These swords which clanked imperiously, also looked several times too large for their carriers who appeared in constant danger of tripping over them. From that day on the two little girls had to stand on a bench between us until they had been noticed and accounted for.

At the end of the first roll-call, the Commandant appeared and read out a list of rules which, when translated, made it abundantly clear that any attempt to escape would be punishable by summary execution and that any complaint about food, conditions or treatment 'would not be made.' It was a gloomy welcome and the mood of the camp slumped dramatically.

There was much else to shed gloom on the motley assembly. The majority were from the Shanghai business community and most of them had been used to a high standard of living. One lady who occupied a room close to ours, had been accustomed to visiting the hairdresser daily to have her hair set. Another who had for years appeared to her friends as a blonde now had to endure as the truth was slowly revealed. The food which came in on a Chinese wheelbarrow, at first seemed quite a treat with pork, potatoes and a few carrots. But lumps of pig fat often with the bristles still attached soon becomes not only unpalatable but indigestible. The water in which we and our vegetables had to wash was brought in the large containers used by the farmers for watering their crops. It came straight from the Grand Canal and the only comforting thing about it was that plant and animal life seemed to thrive in it. Toilet facilities consisted of a row of buckets with seats on top. It fell to someone's lot to empty and clean them out each day. As the hot weather came on the stench was unbearable.

Ken and Godfrey and to a lesser extent, myself, were soon involved medically and here we ran up against unexpected hostility. Apart from the few missionaries in the camp, most people had been used to the best of 'pin-striped trouser' medical attention for which they paid handsomely. Now they had to humble themselves to accept the only care available from the 'bloody young missionaries' as we found ourselves labelled. Missionaries had never ranked high in the business world's estimation. They found it hard to believe we could possibly know what we were doing and their security was seriously undermined.

Ken chose to take on the public health side of camp life and with his gift for cartooning began to produce illustrated instructions about how best to live under these new circumstances which, in our ignorance we thought were funny. They included such basic advice as the constant use of mosquito nets, eating potato skins to get the maximum Vitamin B and being careful to wash our hands before eating and after using the toilets. The response was almost a riot. Several

2222222

blankly refused to use nets over their beds, preferring, apparently to risk malaria and on one black day the usual 'stew' was served up without the vegetables having been washed or scrubbed. It was full of mud and swimming in grease, totally inedible. It was not the cooks who were blamed for this but the doctors who had had the audacity to tell them how to do their jobs. It dawned on us that loss of freedom went very deep and that our throwing our weight about was simply rubbing it in.

A few days after the fateful stew, on Godfrey's birthday, an elderly man who had contracted pneumonia as a result of exposure on the journey up from Shanghai, died. Another man had a haemorrhage from a duodenal ulcer and yet another went berserk threatening to kill the doctors and their children. To make matters worse, the senior nurse in the camp who had been matron in a mission hospital and was a friend of ours, insisted that our two small girls should have some of the food allowed into the camp for the express use of people who were ill. It was true that Betty and I had been increasingly worried that our under two years old had no alternative but to eat the lumps of fat which was dished out to us twice a day. It was with great relief that we accepted small portions of chicken, mashed potatoes and even milk pudding. However this only raised further outcries of 'preferential treatment for the doctors' children'. I think they suspected we were feeding ourselves on it as well.

There were several other children in the camp though none as small as ours and quite early on I was asked to be the mothers' representative on a womens' committee which had been almost immediately organised by one of the more powerful and vocal inmates, Mrs. M. I felt flattered and thought this would be an opportunity to propagate a few of my own ideas on child health but I soon found I had dived into yet another bog of suspicion, mistrust and criticism which left me completely bewildered having never met anything like it before.

One of the great needs for the children was milk in constant supply. Some of the ladies were all for persuading the Japanese to let us have a goat though no one seemed to have much idea of how we would look after it. Having lived, if only for a very short time in the countryside with all its filth and risk of disease, I was less keen. Local goats were not likely to be particularly healthy or clean so I came up with the suggestion that we should ask rather for soya beans out of which we could make soya bean milk as we had in Siaochang for the under-nourished children there and I spoke highly of its nutritious value. This for some reason greatly enraged Mrs. M. who rallied her supporters and brought them to a meeting during which she accused me in eloquent terms of trying to poison them all and being in league with the Japanese. The battle raged backwards and forwards between the goat and the soya bean and the goat won hands down. I could not blame them. Goat's milk would be much pleasanter to take if safe to do so but of course there was no question of the Japanese allowing this to happen so we were no better off. Feeling that the majority did not appreciate my great learning and experience I resigned from the committee leaving it to wallow in its own ignorance. Inside myself I began to realise just how little I knew about human nature and how to deal with the fears which prompted so much of this odd behaviour.

月光之下

CHAPTER 15

RELIEF CAME for us in an unexpected way when Teddy a sixteen year old developed acute appendicitis. The Japanese had planned for a hospital unit to be set up in the largest of the Yangchow camps, 'C' camp which was not yet open. We were not equipped to undertake major surgery but faced with this emergency something had to be done. Between us we possessed one pair of surgical gloves, two pairs of artery forceps, one scalpel and a very small bottle of chloroform.

The whole camp was suddenly galvanised into action. Within two hours of the diagnosis being established a table had been made by Mr. T. a carpenter, a mask for the anaesthetic had been produced out of a piece of wire by Ken, towels, swabs and the handful of instruments had been boiled and the room selected as the operating theatre had been scrubbed from ceiling to floor by hands that were now only too willing to be helpful.

Ken and Godfrey tossed for the privilege of using the scalpel and Godfrey won and put on the one pair of gloves. Ken assisted and one of our own mission nurses, a very experienced theatre nurse, stood by. I gave the anaesthetic, drop by precious drop. Betty stayed with the children and prayed, as did many others. The offending appendix was successfully removed and the patient made an uninterrupted recovery and confidence was established.

As the days went by the walls round the compound seemed to get higher and higher. The only place from which we could glimpse the outside world was the attic window in the main school building. From this one occasionally caught sight of the top of a junk as it sailed by on the Canal and a sideways view of the roof of the magnificent Marco Polo gate away to the south.

The other way was to find an excuse to visit 'C' camp now established in the north east corner of the city about two miles away. Not only did the hospital unit in the new camp have better facilities for medical and surgical care, it also boasted a dentist. The most common excuse therefore for going there was toothache. As toothache is a subjective phenomenon it is difficult to confirm and we could hardly blame the guards for their quite natural surprise at the amount of toothache which developed. It became a common sight to see a group of would-be patients standing outside the guard-house with their mouths wide open awaiting inspection. On one occasion a genuine sufferer was Betty and it hardly seemed fair to laugh when she stood waiting for a none too clean Japanese finger to prod her painful tooth. Her pain proved sufficiently convincing for her to be allowed to join the party.

As doctors Godfrey, Ken and I did rather better by establishing ourselves as specialists in some particular field. There was no question about Godfrey as he had already worked as the Ear, Nose and Throat consultant in Cheloo hospital. Ken had taken on Public Health matters and I with minimum of experience but a great deal of interest, found myself being used as a Cardiologist for the only time in my life. The doctors in the other two camps who were all good friends of ours having worked in the same Mission, took on other roles, one as Consultant Physician, another a Surgeon and a third was an Obstetrician. If the occasion arose and sometimes the excuse was fairly slender, we would send a message requesting a visit from one or other of our colleagues and they in their turn might send for us. Godfrey and Ken were called out on several occasions Godfrey even having to operate one day on a boy in 'C' camp with mastoiditis after an ear infection. There were no adequate instruments in the hospital to deal with such an emergency but Godfrey managed to perform the operation successfully using carpenter's tools and bits of a meccano set. The result was better than many he had done before using proper instruments.

I managed one visit in my new consultative role joining a party going to see the dentist. In spite of our escort of three soldiers, it felt like a day out of school as we pushed our way through the narrow crowded streets with all the familiar sights and smells of a Chinese town. I rather think the more senior doctors in 'C' camp could have managed quite well without me but I carefully examined my patient and solemnly gave my advice and thoroughly enjoyed my day out.

As summer came on, the temperature once more soared to its accustomed heights. It became more and more difficult to face the lumps of pork which seemed to grow more bristles as the days went by. Many people developed fatty diarrhoea and had to stop eating it altogether. The task of keeping the latrines clean and even tolerable to use, did not get easier although Ken and one of the nurses tried to relieve the situation by digging seepage pits for urine.

Nature herself added to our problems by sending a plague of 'stink bugs' into our midst. These were flat, oval-shaped, winged creatures about one and a half inches long. They arrived in their millions like a great black cloud and settled on everything in sight and out of sight. For three days they came. If squashed they emitted a loathsome stench. The only way to deal with them was to sweep them into great heaps and set fire to them. For the few days the plague lasted, a feeling of near kinship grew with our guards who disliked them as much as we did.

The hot weather also brought a change of clothing fashions. Cotton dresses and shorts appeared but the shorts, if worn by females presented a moral dilemma for the Japanese. At first they came down strongly on the side of extreme decency and the order went out that no shorts should be more than one inch above the knee. Ladies knelt on the grass while the exposed expanse of thigh was carefully measured. This phase passed rapidly possibly because shorts began to appear with zig-zag edges to them which made measuring difficult or as it seemed, the Japanese decided it would suit their purposes better if we were left to suffer the consequences of our own decadence. Hems soon went up again.

Summer also brought with it its crop of dandelions—joyful, golden blooms which conjured up memories of home. However these too along with cobwebs came under Japanese scrutiny and were banned. No dandelions or cobwebs would be tolerated.

月
光
之
下

Ken as self-appointed Medical Officer of Health was escorted round to see where these horrors lurked. He took the opportunity to point out to his escort that dandelion leaves were a valuable source of Vitamin C and should be encouraged. Spiders, likewise, performed a salutary duty in that they caught flies and mosquitoes all potential carriers of disease. They too should be left to get on with their job. The Commandant was impressed. When they finally reached the guard house by the gate, Ken's eye lit on a large cobweb hanging high up in a corner and politely pointed this out. The discovery was greeted with guffaws of merriment from the assembled guards and no more was said.

CHAPTER 16

CULTURE IN 'B' camp was noticeably lacking though some talented people did make a few efforts to entertain and amuse. There was an old harmonium in the attic and sometimes in an evening I would take myself up there to play. Often others would wander up and sit around or gaze out of the small window at what view there was.

We had one very good singer in the camp, an attractive young wife who had been separated from her husband for some time before internment. Things were made more difficult for them as the Japanese refused to recognise separation and insisted they go to the same camp. The husband was an older, gentle person who played the violin and still adored his wife. Life must have been almost intolerable at times. They both enjoyed making music and listening to it but I felt I was only adding to his suffering when I agreed to accompany her when she insisted on singing 'I'll walk beside you . . .' a popular song in those days.

We did attempt one jazz session mainly for the benefit of the younger inhabitants. Neither the violin player nor I had much if any sense of 'hot' rhythm but after frantic practising in the attic we did manage to produce quite an effective rendering of 'In the Mood.' The leader of the band was a youth who played the harmonica at the same time banging an empty suitcase with a block of wood attached to one foot.

Our main source of excitement was the monthly arrival of food parcels. Before being interned we had been told we could leave money with neutral friends in Shanghai or with the International Red Cross who undertook to pack and deliver standard size parcels to the various camps. Our own missionary society had funds sufficient to provide all of us, three hundred or so, with parcels for six months. We were not too worried about this as no one expected the war to last much longer than that. It was like Christmas each month as we dived into our parcels and pulled out small tins of tomato puree, lard, Nescafé and jam. There was usually a packet of cigarettes which being non-smokers we were able to barter for jam or coffee. The total quantity did not amount to much but it made all the difference to our diet. Elizabeth's favourite meal was bread, now baked in 'C' camp, with lard spread on it. The jam was our one source of sweetness and it mattered little that the label described it as 'apricot jam made from the finest selected strawberries.'

When the seventh lot of parcels was due we kept well out of the way to avoid the envy we expected to feel when there was nothing for us. To our amazement our own parcels kept on coming and continued to do so to the end of the war. Only after it was all over did we hear that when the mission funds ran out, a Chinese business man in Hankow had stepped in to finish the job.

Communication with the outside world was almost totally lacking and we had no idea at all of how the war was going. We were allowed to write a twenty-five word letter each per month on official Red Cross forms with space on the back for a reply. A handful of them got through and an even smaller handful ever came back. Even then many of the twenty-five words we or our families wrote would be heavily censored and scored out.

During the summer word went round that we were to be visited by the Swiss Consul who had taken responsibility for Allied interests. He was to have an interview with the Commandant and with the doctors in the Commandant's presence. Many people prepared what they wanted to say but the subject matter was severely restricted by the Commandant. Ken and Godfrey were inundated with messages and letters for friends in Shanghai and they themselves had prepared a report which they hoped to be able to smuggle somehow into the hands of the Consul. We could at least voice our dissatisfaction over food, water and medical supplies even if nothing ever came of it.

The day came and the Consul arrived. The group to meet him sat around a table in the Commandant's office, the Consul asking and receiving non-commital replies. The Commandant, Mr. Y. was a pleasant kindly man who had himself experienced a short time of internment in Australia but he, like us, came ultimately under the authority of the military and so had to watch his own step carefully. At one point, however, the telephone rang and the Commandant left the table to answer it and possibly deliberately, stood with his back to the others in the room. Ken felt a kick on his foot and caught the eye of the Consul as he nodded towards his open brief case which he held under the table. Letters and requests were bundled silently in and all was calm again as the Commandant returned to his seat.

He, the Commandant, however, could not always be taken for granted. At one point during this hot summer the heat in the kitchen became almost unbearable and Ken decided to put in two vents in the roof to let some of the heat escape. The Commandant was away but his second in command gave permission for this to be done. On his return the Commandant was furious with Ken and shouted at him for half an hour. It may just have been a show of authority as no expected punishment of Ken or the camp was forthcoming.

月光之下

Various dramatic incidents occurred during this time. A seventeen year old girl nearly died with malaria. Her temperature rose to 107°F and nurses worked round the clock sponging her down with water. Two days later, Olga, one of the several White Russians in camp tried to commit suicide. She had fallen in love with the Roman Catholic priest, also interned, and seeing no happy solution to her problem, she had taken sodium amytal tablets which she had brought with her from Shanghai. She was bitterly angry with the doctors for resuscitating her.

Yet another 'incident' occurred at roll call in which the children were involved. Roll call happened twice a day and took a variable amount of time. We were alway lined up in blocks of ten by ten to make calculation easier for the counters. Margie and Elizabeth were quite used to this and usually stood fairly quietly with us. On this particular day, however, it was unusually hot and there was no shade. It was some time before anyone came to count us and the children began to get restless and fretful. Godfrey picked up Margie and Ken took Elizabeth in his arms while we went on standing in the eye of the sun for what seemed an interminable length of time. Once again the guards found they were two short in their reckoning. They counted and recounted with mounting anger and excitement. Two ladies in the front row fainted which necessitated the children being transferred to Betty and me while our husbands attended to them. We could not attract the guards' attention as on convincing themselves that two had escaped and not having been with us on previous occasions when the same thing had happened, they had dashed off in various directions to search the grounds and look for evidence from the surrounding walls and it was a much as our lives were worth to leave the spot on which we were standing to go after them. Their final discomfiture at discovering their mistake was just as alarming. Betty and I removed ourselves from the scene with the children as quickly as we could.

CHAPTER 17

BY SEPTEMBER the food situation had seriously deteriorated. Often the bread which was baked in 'C' camp and was the most valuable part of our rations, failed to arrive as did any form of meat so we were reduced to tea, without milk of course, plus mushy narrow. Guerilla warfare in the surrounding countryside prevented food entering the city. Without the monthly food parcels we would have been in a bad way. This may have been one of the factors which made the Japanese decide to move us back to an area where supplies were better and transport easier. It had also become more possible for them to do this as there had been a further repatriation of American civilians and this had left spaces in some of the Shanghai camps. Betty had once again been offered the chance to go home and once again turned it down to my great relief but it wasn't an easy decision for her.

The first we knew of any move was a notice in Japanese which was pinned up on a notice board. For several days it stayed there, no one taking any notice of it. Then the Commandant summoned the camp representatives plus Godfrey and Ken to his office where he informed them that the notice was telling us of our transfer to Shanghai camps and that the move was now, thanks to our lack of inquisitiveness, only days away and our beds and heavy luggage needed to be ready by the next day. There followed a few hours of hectic sorting and packing and with some apprehension we watched our precious belongings and especially our beds, vanish through the gate. For the next three nights we slept, or tried to, on the floor. Grass was collected to make 'nests' for the children which they thought was great fun especially when they found that grass was nice stuff to throw at each other or their parents. Godfrey and Betty lay on one side of them, Ken and I on the other. By now the nights were beginning to get chilly and we only had our coats to cover ourselves with.

The Commandant had asked the doctors to help him sort people out into two groups. The elderly, unfit, and children were, as far as accommodation allowed, to go to one of the better camp sites situated in College buildings while the younger and physically fit would be put in the notorious camp in Pootung in which so far only unattached men had been housed. The family camps were already adequately provided with doctors and nurses but the one in Pootung had lost some through repatriation and he asked Ken and Godfrey whether they would be prepared to fill the gaps. Families were being kept together so it would mean all or none. If he had ordered us to go we would have had no choice but to obey but he knew more about Pootung than we did at that point and was gracious enough to leave the decision to us. We discussed it at length but all felt we should accept his suggestion, and although the pressures and unpleasantnesses of

月光之下

the early days had lessened, we could not help feeling some relief at the thought of a possibly more vigorous community with less emotional demands. In fact we looked on it as quite an adventure. Our two small girls were the only children in our party.

On the day of departure we were each given hard-boiled eggs and some bread to feed on till we reached Pootung. We were lined up in four columns in the front garden complete with all our hand baggage and at a given signal the gate was ceremoniously opened and we marched through it back along the streets to the Marco Polo gate and down to the Grand Canal. Just being outside the high wall of the camp compound was enouth to raise most people's spirits even if it was a false illusion of freedom. Tied up by the bank of the Canal were several quite respectable river boats to take us down to Chinkiang on the far side of the Yangtse from whence we had sailed six months earlier. This time it was an exciting trip for Margie and Elizabeth now over two years old, and as the weather was good we were all able to enjoy our day out as we passed numerous junks and barges wending their stately way along the Canal and the villages dotted along the bank where life seemed to be going on as it always had done over the centuries. The only thing to mar this part of the journey was that one of the men in the party suddenly produced a strangulated hernia which gave him very severe pain and needed immediate hospital attention. It was impossible to make the boat go any faster but as soon as we docked at the quay side in Chekiang he was whisked off to the nearest hospital. As far as we knew he recovered but the event caused some gloom amongst the rest of us especially as it had meant separation for his wife who had to travel on with us.

Elizabeth, who up to that time had never seen a boy as small as herself, was intrigued by a Japanese one standing with his father on the quayside. She went straight up to him, poked him in the tummy and said, 'Mummy, what's this?' The little boy stared back at her equally puzzled, and we left him staring after us as we were once more herded into lines for the forced march to the station.

Ahead of us stretched another night journey and after three nights on the floor we were all more than ready to sleep but the seats were wooden and we were packed like sardines. There was nowhere for the children to sit except on our laps and they were now the age when keeping still for more than a few seconds becomes a physical impossibility. They wanted to run up and down the coach but being caught by an angry guard once was enough and we struggled to keep them within the confines of our legs. It was still daylight when we left Chekiang but the blinds were down and a sharp Japanese bark reminded us that we were not allowed to peep out of the windows which also had to be kept firmly shut. All night long heavy army boots marched incessantly up and down the length of the train making sure that nobody stayed asleep for too long.

Sometime during the morning we drew into an empty siding at the back of one of Shanghai's stations where buses were waiting to take us to the Bund. Although we were extremely tired and anything but free, it was a relief to be back on more familiar ground. Also

45

to our delight, our driver was Chinese and only too ready to talk which he did freely as there had not been enough guards to go round all the buses and we were for the first time free of their surveillance. He caught us up with the war and we learned that Italy had changed sides and was now an ally and for a brief spell we felt like returning exiles as Chinese in the streets, waved as we passed and Russian police on duty at crossroads waved to us. Anti-British propaganda for all its vehemence did not appear to have achieved much and we were quite moved by our reception by the locals.

As we boarded the open ferry waiting for us at the famous Customs jetty, our eyes caught sight of large ship lying on its side in the middle of the river, half of its hull above the water. This we learned was the *Conte Verdi* the luxury Italian liner which had been used to ferry repatriating foreigners between Shanghai and Lorenco Marques in East Africa. When Italy capitulated she had been caught in Shanghai and had been promptly scuttled by her crew. The ferry took us close to her bows and, clearly visible on her upturned hull, was the small figure of a Japanese soldier with legs apart and his rifle at his side. At his feet stood a very small electric fan, presumably one of his lawful perks on its way home.

By the time we disembarked and in spite of all the excitement, Elizabeth had fallen asleep in my arms. A two-year old, even if not up to normal size, is no light weight and by the time we had been rounded up once more, counted several times and marched with our luggage the mile or so along the narrow road between tall factory buildings all shuttered and barred with weeds growing high along the railway tracks running parallel to the road, I felt as though my arms, not would break, but were already broken. Every time I see refugees trudging across endless miles with children in their arms, my arms ache again.

CHAPTER 18

WE KNEW we could not expect five-star accommodation to be awaiting us but even so we were not quite prepared for the sight which met our eyes as we rounded a bend in the road. The huge, grimy, red-brick building which loomed in sight looked like a prison which, of course, it now was. It had clearly come into its own. There were three storeys of it, punctuated by large and mostly broken windows patched with paper, and surrounded by a high brick wall and barbed wire.

For years since it had been condemned as a warehouse, it had been used as a coal dump so when the first batch of internees had arrived they had to spend their days clearing the piles

月光之下

of coal dust which covered the ground floor windows. The coal dust, true to its nature, had impregnated every corner of the building.

The all male occupants had not believed the Japanese when they first announced that they would be introducing women to the camp. It was not until they were ordered to clear certain rooms to accommodate females and married couples that they took the matter seriously. There then followed much washing of shirts and shaving of faces and as we approached the gate every window had several male faces peering out at us apparently eager for their first glimpse in nine months of us glamorous creatures. There were about two hundred women in our group of four hundred or so and we were joining another eight hundred men left behind in Pootung. In our party was a handful of teenage girls but even they and certainly the rest of us, must have looked far from glamorous at that moment dropping as we were from tiredness, untidy and very hungry.

In spite of the way we looked, the welcome could not have been warmer. Just inside the oppressively large gate was the camp band, saxophone, trumpet, clarinet and double bass putting on their hottest 'jam' for our benefit. It was very heart-warming if a trifle overwhelming at that moment. There too were the friends we had seen off from the Country Club all those months before, looking a bit thinner as indeed we all were.

As I walked through the rather ominous looking gate past the soldiers on sentry duty, the clear thought came into my mind—'This is the next bit of life to be lived. Get on and live it.' Suddenly it was no longer just a waste of time, an interruption of normal valuable activity or a terrifying and uncertain interlude in our lives, but life itself and the next step for the four of us. This was still very much in my mind as we were ushered into a large room with great solid wooden pillars and a brick floor. Here we were given welcome cups of tea, without milk of course, and as we thankfully drank this, having to blow the children's till it was cool enough for them, the British representative delivered an address of welcome. Then we were shown to our rooms. The Gales and ourselves were determined not to be separated if we could help it and we joined a group of other husbands and wives to be taken up an outside flight of concrete steps and into the main building at first floor level. Through a wide opening on our left we found ourselves in another vast space, this time empty apart from the two rows of wooden pillars with racks between them for storage purposes. The pillars reached twenty feet up into the ceiling.

At the far end was another wide door at one side of which was a wooden staircase and on the other an elevator. This left a small corner by the far window. We could not imagine how we could possibly settle in anywhere with the two children. The space allowed for each person was seven feet by three feet. By the time the couples with us had taken up their allotted spaces there was nothing left for us but the corner by the window. At that moment all we wanted was somewhere to lie down and get some sleep. The children were crying and irritable and our hearts, warmed by the welcome now began to cool down rapidly. But we were among friends, one of whom was the senior doctor, a member of our own mission. He offered us the use of a

月
光
之
下

spare bed in the eight-bedded ward of the so-called hospital and there we put the small girls, one at each end and within seconds they were both sound asleep.

The only other available accommodation in the hospital area was the dentist's chair so that night and for the next few nights, Betty and I took it in turns to sleep in this, while the other slept, or tried to, on the camp's only stretcher on the floor. Godfrey and Ken were banished to a cold, dark corner in the other building where they attempted to get some sleep on a concrete floor. As no luggage had arrived no one had any blankets and only the contents of their hand luggage to cover or pad themselves with. Someone kindly lent Ken a coat to put under him.

Meanwhile the problem of where to put us remained until someone had the bright idea of raising the elevator to the second floor and flooring in the lift shaft below it thus adding an almost equal space to the window corner of the room in which forty-two couples were now established. With the doors of the lift a new floor was created and a partition put up between us and the rest of the dormitory. With the ceiling twenty feet up this could only shut us off partially from the main room but hopefully it would keep out some of the children's noise and give them a modicum of privacy. The elevator itself became a room for another couple and we were assured that it was perfectly safe and could not possibly come down. The Gales were the ones to whose lot it fell to sleep underneath it and gazing up at its bottom with its many cross beams, Betty wondered whether one morning she would wake to find herself a waffle. To reassure her the men unscrewed the metal lift slides and bent them across underneath the hovering potential waffle iron thus giving an impression, albeit a false one, of security.

We now inherited a space, thirteen feet by nine. This was slightly reduced in practical terms by the greasy uprights on which the elevator had run and the oily cables which hung down each side of the shaft. However this was made up for by our day-bed which now came fully into its own. Folded up by day it gave a good space under the window in which the children could play or have a bath in the canvas bath which Godfrey had inherited from his pioneering father. Fully extended at night, the bed occupied the whole space between the partition and Elizabeth's cot which had been constructed out of an old play-pen. As a settee it was the only comfortable piece of furniture in the whole camp and over the next two years people were to visit us just for the privilege of sitting on it.

Ken, who wasted no time in exploring the place, very soon rounded up enough wood to create a table for us which folded back under the window when not in use and a combined table and bench seats for the Gale family which turned upside down could slide under their beds at night.

It was a good week before our luggage and beds actually turned up. Many of the trunks and cases had been turned out and ransacked, their remaining contents mixed up so causing great confusion and argument over what belonged to who. Almost everyone had lost valuable winter clothing or blankets which could be ill-spared. However with the arrival of what was left, the business of settling in began in earnest. Space was carefully measured out and in no

49

time at all, marked out by a variety of curtains, blankets, sheets, bedspreads, anything which could give a pretence of privacy. A passageway was kept open between the pillars and walking along it was often possible to get a glimpse of life behind the curtains. Some remained pretty and immaculate right through while others never rose above the status of slum. Ours came somewhere in between. It was rarely tidy and, wash as we would, we never succeeded in getting rid of the coal dust.

The one great advantage of our room was the view. Broken and filthy though it was, the window looked out over factory roofs to the Whangpoo river and the famous Shanghai skyline. In the middle of the river we could see the stricken *Conte Verdi* and during the next twelve months part of our entertainment lay in watching intrigued as the Japanese, with their usual skilful manoeuvering, set about raising her inch by inch from her muddy bed until she sat upright once more in midstream.

The window faced west and as the sun set over the city each evening it became quite a ritual with the children to send our love by it to our families over whom in a few hours' time it would be rising.

CHAPTER 19

OUR ROOM-MATES were as mixed a bag of humans as you could hope to meet. Mrs. S. looked as smart the day she walked out of camp as she did the day she arrived and her cubicle was always immaculate and pretty. Her husband too, never seemed to have a hair out of place. Their near neighbours lived in a perpetual slum. There was the same variety throughout the camp, a factor which would make it so different from a prisoner of war camp. We had a Bishop, the mainly negro crew of a scuttled American ship and two ex-Sing Sing convicts. Every shade of colour was represented, anyone claiming American, British or Dutch nationality was included as were a few pathetically stateless people including a German who had been picked up by the Japanese on the streets of Shanghai. He claimed to have come off a German warship on shore leave but was not wearing uniform and could produce no evidence of nationality. He was a great gorilla of a man and understandably felt out of place in this Allied community. However he established himself as a useful member of the camp by collecting every odd thing he could lay his hands on, nails, buttons, washers. All found their way to his corner and he was quite prepared to sell them to the highest bidder.

月光之下

One of the greatest delights of our new home, especially to the children, was the discovery that we now had proper toilets with chains that pulled. Our delight was short-lived. The four toilets at the end of our room had to serve all the two hundred women and the only time there was no queue was in the middle of the night. The seats which were already broken when we arrived, soon had to be removed for public health reasons. The chains were continually breaking and the concrete floor was always wet. Summer brought its own problems with frequent tummy upsets among the inmates and in winter the intense cold added to the misery. On one occasion soon after we arrived, while closeted I found myself quite unconsciously humming a nostalgic tune from 'The Immortal Hour.' When I emerged, a tall, artistic looking lady to whom I had not yet spoken, came out of the queue to throw her arms round me and say, 'I never expected to hear that in this filthy place.'

Life soon began to settle once more into something of a routine. At 8.30 a.m. Ken or Godfrey would go down to the room set aside as a Common Room in a building joined to the main one by a bridge onto which our dormitory opened. Here he would collect our mugs of tea and the day's ration of bread. This amounted to a very small loaf, wholemeal fortunately, per person. How it was made we never fathomed and since I have taken to making my own bread I have wondered even more. Frequently when we cut into it we would find it consisted of a thick, slimy, ropy substance, difficult to slice and more difficult to eat because of its sourness. Quite often a whole loaf would have to be abandoned for use as fuel in the kitchen. But when it was good it was very welcome as the one item of food which Elizabeth would eat with any relish. Margie consumed anything that was put in front of her.

At 9 a.m. we trooped outside for roll-call. When the men had first arrived in the camp the only available outside space was the roadway surrounding the main building. Then the Japanese had opened up an area which had once been part of a village but reduced to rubble during the attack on Shanghai in 1937. They surrounded this area with two lots of barbed wire with a few feet in between and had erected watch towers at intervals round the perimeter. The whole space was wide open with no tree or growing thing in sight. The men had been set to clearing a space about the size of a football pitch on which over a thousand people could be lined up for counting and the rest the men had themselves turned into small plots of ground in which by the time we arrived, all manner of small plants and even some vegetables were growing. One plot furthest from the building had nothing growing in it but the earth had been trodden flat by the feet of the camp's piper, a Scottish engineer who, regardless of heat or cold could be seen marching back and forth with his pipes. Whatever his other clothing might or might not be, his Glengarry was always on his head. His proud boast was that he had once played at Balmoral by Royal command. He was a great gift to the camp and a bonus for us in that he permitted the children to use the hallowed piece of ground to play in when he was not using it.

Roll call was always a solemn and often frightening affair. Punctually at 9 a.m. the old factory fire alarm bell would shriek through the building jerking us all to our feet and following us as we grabbed the children and dashed out to the playing field. We were allowed three minutes from the moment the bell started to ring.

As soon as we were all lined up the Japanese flag, affectionately known to us as the 'poached egg', was raised above the Commandant's office and the Commandant would come out of his office on to the balcony and along with the assembled guards and their commanding officer would bow reverently to it while we stood motionless at attention. We did realise that for them this was a religious ceremony and during it I would sometimes think of our friends in Japan and the soldiers we had entertained in Siaochang and pray for them all. It certainly helped to relieve the apprehension we always felt at the these times.

The ceremony over the counting would begin. A group of guards would march up and down the lines of internees and their barking and punching made it abundantly clear that we should stand with the palms of our hands flat against our sides, our feet together and no expression on our faces. This I found very difficult especially with Betty, an inveterate humourist at my side. Most Japanese though by no means all, tend to be fairly short and for the smaller ones their ancestral swords dangling at their sides often looked close to tripping them up. Most Americans and British appear large and ungainly by the side of a neat Japanese and under these conditions they looked larger than usual and as the days went by, more and more scruffy in an increasingly odd assortment of clothes. This sight combined with the solemnity of the occasion often got the better of us and on one such time an uncontrollable grin on my face brought a sharp reminder of my position in the form of a punch from a Japanese fist aimed at the pit of my stomach which almost sent me flying.

Each morning the doctors had to provide a list of those in bed or unfit to come out. A soldier then had to be escorted round the various rooms and the hospital to make sure the list was telling the truth. The rest of us had to wait while this was being done.

Once roll call was over we were free to do as we liked. Our husbands would take themselves off to the hospital to see patients while Betty and I did our best with the means at our disposal to clean up our cubicle and amuse the children. The latter was not difficult as they very quickly discovered friends in the surrounding dormitories who seemed only too ready to entertain them, and be entertained by them.

Laundry was a problem. The Japanese had built long wash troughs supplied at intervals with tap water from the river. Unfortunately they had built them to Japanese specifications and for the taller of us it was backbreaking work. They also supplied something which they called soap but we never experienced any lather with it. It's main use was to provide food for hungry rats.

Lunch round about midday consisted of a bowl of soup with bits of white cabbage floating in it, accompanied by rice. This had the great advantage for us of being unpolished but not only did it retain its Vitamin B, it also contained many of its husks and had also lain in store long enough for the rats to get to know it and in addition to eating it, leaving their calling cards

月光之下

scattered among the grains. The evening meal was similar, coming after evening roll call. The only difference being a few more bits of white cabbage and occasionally a little meat and a few lumps of potato. For a while we were also provided with a supply of 'cracked wheat.' This had been sent to China from America during one of China's many famine times but sadly the Chinese did not know how to use it so it had lain in store for years. The rats had not found it or had been unable to reach it but whatever animal produces weevils had made their home in it. In one bowlful alone I once counted fifty two fat weevils. They blended in well with the cracked wheat and as long as no one was rash enough to draw attention to them we managed to eat without noticing and they probably provided a very much needed source of protein in our meagre diet.

Whenever the meal appeared Elizabeth would start howling. The only food she would accept readily was the meat and potato. Confucius is reputed to have said that 'a mother seeing her child eat, had no need of food herself.' All I can say is that Confucius was never a hungry mother picking out precious morsels from her own dish to put into her child's gaping mouth.

Evening of course brought darkness. The only room to be lit up was the Common Room which was blacked out with huge matting screens over the windows. The only other lights in the camp were dim, heavily shaded pilot lights at each end of the dormitories under which groups of people wanting a quieter life, would cluster like moths to read their books.

And so to bed. All was well, provided the children slept and the Japanese had no cause to punish the camp by getting everyone out of bed in the small hours for an extra roll call in our various rooms. This was their favourite punishment and after considerable pleading, the children were excused attendance and either Betty or I were permitted to stay with them. Margie as well as being a good eater, was also a good sleeper. Elizabeth had a way of waking in the middle of the night and crying. I had to shove my hand through the bars of her cot as rapidly as I could as if she went on crying she could wake about three hundred people in the surrounding rooms. I would have to hold her hand until she dropped off to sleep again which sometimes took a long time. Fortunately in our confined space I could reach her without getting out of bed so at least on bitter winter nights, it was only my left arm which froze.

CHAPTER 20

THE WARMTH of our reception and the meeting of so many old friends gave us an initial feeling of almost being on holiday after the struggles of Yangchow. However we were very soon made aware of the true state of things in the camp. The past nine months it seemed, had been anything but easy. The filth, the food, the separation from wives and families had brought out the worst in many of the men. We learned of attempted suicides and attempted murders, theft and violence. On one occasion when 'ribbon fish', whatever that is, was fed to the camp, there was a riot which was only subdued when the Japanese brought in machine guns.

Much of the trouble was caused by a gang of men who had styled themselves the camp police. They commandeered a small hut which they called their 'office' and from here they ruled the camp. The Japanese, apart from making sure no one got out, were unconcerned about the internal running of the place which was left to the internees, so this left the gang a free hand to do as they pleased. They put their own friends into the kitchen to handle the food as it arrived in the camp and with these men taking their 'perks' it was doubtful how much of the ration the rest ever received. Extra food could be bought by selling some other commodity anyone might be lucky enough to possess.

It was not many days before we ourselves became aware of these men. I found myself feeling more afraid of them than of the Japanese. But even they could hardly be blamed for all the pilfering that went on. One could never be sure that a garment hung out to dry in the morning would still be there at the end of the day. They may not have been entirely to blame for the illegitimate babies which began to appear as the months went by but it was at least suspected that the police office after the arrival of our contingent, was used as a brothel. We had brought in with us a number of teenage girls, several of them Eurasians, beautiful and vulnerable.

Quite apart from the so-called police, the rest of us were quite capable of producing our own problems. In such an atmosphere of frustration, hunger, discomfort and above all, doubt and fear about the future, this was hardly surprising. It was not the big things which got us down but the petty irritations of life. If the Japanese were being more than usually difficult or if there was an air raid, as there frequently was in later months, we responded magnificently. But if someone pushed their bed an inch or two into their neighbour's space or someone opened a window—or shut it—all hell was let loose. A lady from one of the women's rooms came to me one day and asked me to give a message to another woman. 'But,' I said, 'she sleeps in the next bed to you.' 'Oh yes,' came the answer, 'but we're not speaking.'

月光之下

With men outnumbering women by about three to one, all the heavy cleaning as well as the cooking, was done by them. All the women had to do was to look after their own cubicles. This was hardly enough to fill even an hour of their time and there is little more likely to cause trouble than unemployed women in a confined space. Many were outstanding knitters and sweaters were knitted up, worn for a few days, unravelled and knitted up again. This can become tedious. Even Bridge and Mahjong can hardly be played all day. Many found relief, as women will, in gossip. As I passed one small group one day I heard one say, clearly revelling in her spicy news, 'Did you see Mr. S. sitting on Mrs. A's bed last night?'

For us things were easier. The men had plenty to do anyway and Betty and I had the children to look after. But for two Mums to bring up their children in a small corner with no escape is no easy matter and leaves plenty of room for trouble. Betty is a nurse and I am only a doctor. It is well known that nurses' standards are far higher than doctors'. I thought she was too fussy at times and she was sure I was not fussy enough. I am quite prepared to believe she was right. We did have our arguments followed by awkward periods of not knowing how to talk to each other. This, when there is no way of getting away from each other, can be uncomfortable.

As doctors too, we once again found ourselves the targets of suspicion and again this came mainly from the women. There were many who had been in 'A' camp in Yangchow who had not known us and even those who had were still not too sure of us. Every now and again extra food would find its way into the camp. This was usually dried milk or eggs. It was like gold. Of course the first people to benefit were any patients who might be in hospital or seriously needing special diets. Once their needs had been met there was little to distribute any further. The burning question always arose as to who should get whatever there was. Should it go to the oldest, the youngest or the adolescents? One fourteen year old was quite clear in her own mind. She said apologetically to a friend of ours who had just about reached her forties, 'I really feel we should get it because, you see, you are at the end of your life and we're just at the beginning of ours.'

Whoever did eventually get it, it was always suspected by some that the doctors, who had the final say, pinched the bulk of it for their children. There were times when we wished we could.

On other occasions it was medicines which caused trouble. They were hard enough to come by as it was, numerous representations having to be made to the Japanese for necessary supplies. Some things we never did get, but for some reason, it was I who roused the suspicions of a certain lady who accused me to my face of hoarding Cascara tablets, something I never actually needed myself. Others were convinced I kept a secret store of sanitary towels. Would that I had. The lack of such commodities along with the filth of the toilets was the cause of much day to day misery.

I remember someone once tried to bribe me with a small tin of coffee to give her what she needed and I know she disbelieved me when I insisted that I could not help her. I accepted the coffee as though it was given in good faith but it did her no good.

A great source of frustration was the lack of adequate contact between the camp and the Commandant. At the outset two men were appointed to represent the Americans and British respectively. The British one was a quiet older man chosen because he had lived in Japan and knew the language, but, probably because he knew the Japanese better than most of us, he was loath to put forward any request which he felt they might not like and which might cause trouble. There were many urgently needed things, basic tools like screwdrivers and nails, paper for the older children who would be having lessons and, to us most important of all, medical supplies.

The Commandant was a reasonable man though less approachable than the one we had over us in Yangchow, but he too had his problems. Although theoretically in control, the patrolling of the camp and the discipline was in the hands of the guards' commanding officer, and he too had to watch his step. All the guards were soldiers who had seen at least three years' active service. They may have been wounded or were medically unfit to continue. All of them disliked their job and felt this assignment was something of a disgrace. To avoid fraternisation with us the personnel was constantly changing and always within the twenty or more would be at least two who were members of the notorious Military Police and planted there to keep an eye, not only on us, but on their fellow soldiers and their brutality was not limited to their enemies. This of course, made the guard Commander even more anxious to keep us all on our toes.

In this atmosphere of fear and uncertainty it was hardly surprising that people tended to keep themselves to themselves, jealously guarding their precious possessions and their privacy such as it was.

CHAPTER 21

IT DID NOT take many days after our arrival to realise that we had landed in a potentially inflammable situation and that many changes needed to be brought about. The question was how it should be done and none of us felt inclined any more to try telling other people how they ought to behave. We decided to wait and trust that God would show us how He would like things done in His own good time. Meanwhile we just got on with the business of living and trying to get to know people.

月光之下

There were already bright spots in the camp. We soon began to pick out individuals with spirits which even the most miserable of circumstances failed to dampen. There was Mr. D. the self-appointed leader of the sanitary squad who gaily led his band of merry men round the lavatories whistling and joking as they cleaned up the mess and sluiced down the floors, everlastingly and uncomplainingly clearing blocked drains and mending broken chains as best they could. There were the Cohens, a Jewish family with four children who were always ready to do anything that needed doing and the way they lived as a family all the way through was like a fire to warm your hands at. When the youngest reached his twelfth birthday the whole camp rejoiced with him in his excitement at celebrating his Bar Mitzvah, wearing his little black cap for the first time and going off to pray in a secluded corner with the other Jewish men.

There were the all-black crew members of an American ship which had scuttled itself off the China coast rather than be taken by the Japanese. A group of these built an outside brick stove on which we could re-heat our rations or even create dishes and even cakes of sorts out of the bits and pieces which came in our monthly Red Cross parcels. Not only did they keep the stove going but they also provided a constant stream of wit. Once when a white woman was complaining about the weather which, being unbearably hot and dry had turned to rain, one of them said, 'Lady, de good Lawd don't know how ter please yer.'

There were Ivy and Anne and 'Ginger' all members of our own Mission who lived three rooms away from us but were always ready to receive two small visitors at any time of day. Amongst other things they made a fully furnished dolls' house for Margie and Elizabeth out of cardboard boxes which was a source of great activity and delight.

We became aware of many other individuals, the majority in fact, living inoffensive lives and keeping the peace but in spite of them the basic problems remained and affected the whole atmosphere of the camp. Answers began to emerge in an unexpected way.

Godfrey and Ken were immediately involved with the other doctor, Keith, in seeing patients and regular clinic times were established. For many people there was little they could offer in the way of treatment but the small hospital with its little cubicles for consulting rooms, was the only place in the whole camp in which it was possible to have a conversation without being overheard and even here one had to keep one's voice down. So coming to the doctor did, as it so often does in general practice, offer people a chance not only to bring their physical ills but to unburden themselves of a variety of fears and problems some of which had haunted them for years. The fact that time was unlimited made this all the more possible.

One of the first patients to come through Ken's hands was a senior business man whose wife had been repatriated some weeks before he was interned. They had parted on a sour note leaving Mr. G. feeling desolate and guilty with no way of contacting her to put things right even if he could have seen how. One day on a table in a hotel lounge in Shanghai, he had found a book with the intriguing title, 'For Sinners Only.' No one seemed to own it so he picked it up and read it. It was a book published in the '30s about the work of the Oxford Group which was very active in Europe at that time even alarming Hitler's Gestapo. With its stories of faith and reconciliation through people becoming different it was for Mr. G. like a light being switched on. He began to put into practice the things it talked about and went into camp feeling almost buoyant with hope.

Strangely enough, Ken, Godfrey and I had all met the Group in different parts of Britain when we were students and had learned from it the secret of the kind of praying which includes listening to God as well as talking. Eric Liddell too had had a similar experience. One evening Ken was asked to give a lecture on Chinese art and something he said made Mr. G. feel that here at last was someone who would understand what he had been through. When he found that indeed we did know, he greeted us like members of his own family.

Mr. G. had another unexpected side to his nature which included a fascination for the habits of fleas which he had studied in depth. His knowledge was to prove invaluable. If a rat was caught it had to be taken to Mr. G. immediately before it cooled down and the fleas left it. Mr. G. then removed a flea for examination under a microscope and if it turned out to be the type of flea which feeds on sewer rats which carry plague, then the whole camp was galvanised into a rat-catching orgy. Normally we tended to accept rats as our companions in misery.

Soon after we met Mr. G. he became seriously ill with bronchopneumonia and with no adequate means of looking after him the outlook seemed very poor. He was in bed in his own dormitory where there were plenty of men in surrounding beds only too pleased to care for him. One evening he was so much worse that Ken was summoned by one of his friends. When Ken reached his bedside, Mr. G. asked him to pray for his wife and daughter as he did not expect to see them again. Ken did this and as Mr. G. seemed to relax and to be resting peacefully left him in the hands of his friends. Ken naturally told us how ill Mr. G. was and we all prayed for him.

The next day Mr. G. got out of bed apparently perfectly well. He found Ken and said, 'Look what's happened!' There could be no doubting the miracle of his recovery and in his delight at still being alive he was eager to know how he could help in sorting out the camp's many problems. Ken suggested they should meet in the early morning with one or two others to think and ask for God's guidance about these things.

They were a mixed group. One was a river pilot who had run away from home as a youth. Another was a highly respectable architect and another a Jewish businessman. One was an accountant.

Meetings of more than three people at a time were strictly forbidden except in the Common room where the Japanese could keep an eye on us if they wanted to but under the stairs almost opposite the main gate of the camp was a large cupboard and in this they decided to meet. They chose 8 a.m. as a good time when it was reckoned the sentry at the end of his twelve hour shift by the gate would be losing interest in his work and there was an hour to go before his relief would take over.

The men approached singly, carrying towels as though they were making for the fire hydrants at which they usually did their washing. For Ken and Godfrey it was a convenient

月光之下

meeting place as it was just below our room though even then it meant going outside and passing close to the guard-house to reach it. For the others it meant a walk round the outside of the main building but none was ever caught. Occasionally Betty or I would join them but it was decided that, for the sake of the children, we should stay in our rooms and do our praying there as best we could.

These morning meetings soon acquired a pattern. The men would discuss the main problems and then sit in silence waiting for God's thoughts as to what He would like done about them. It was a totally practical approach and one in which Mr. J. the Jew, could happily participate. The thoughts which emerged were equally practical. The problem uppermost in their minds to begin with was that of the camp 'police' and the idea came to replace them with a fresh lot of incorruptible men. Knowing the type of people they were up against this seemed a good but virtually impossible and distinctly dangerous thing to do. However they went ahead and drew up a list of men known for their integrity as well as physical bulk. Everyone was sworn to secrecy to such an extent that even Betty and I did not have any idea of what was going on. A number of old red armbands we had worn while in Shanghai were deftly rounded up and a woman known for her sewing skills was asked to sew 'Police' in white lettering on them. She too was sworn to secrecy.

One morning as we emerged from the building to go out for roll call, there at every vantage point along the route to the exercise ground was a large, impressive man, red armband on his left arm and hands behind his back looking as though he had never done anything else. There was one outside the kitchen where people left their thermos flasks to collect boiled water for drinking and tooth washing, another by the queue of pails lined up by the tap for laundry water and others by the laundry troughs and drying lines, all potential pilfering points. Seventy-nine of these stalwarts were recruited for policing duties, twice the number of the original 'gang'.

We waited for the explosion when the others realised what was happening but none came. The so-called police who had wielded such frightening power in the camp seemed to vanish rather as did our friends the rats when adequately chased. The police 'office' was abandoned forthwith without comment from anyone. We could only imagine that they thought this was some new order from the Japanese and as for the Japanese themselves, they could not really care less how we organised ourselves as long as there was no trouble so there was no comment from them, and roll call proceeded as though nothing had happened. The first hurdle had been jumped.

59

CHAPTER 22

THE ATMOSPHERE in the camp changed dramatically almost overnight. One was suddenly more aware of everyone else and with the new feeling of security there was a general air of relaxation, but more remained to be sorted out. The problems of food distribution, perhaps the most urgent, and the whole question of improving our contact with the Commandant. The little group of men went on meeting in the early morning to think about these things and the number finally grew to seventeen.

No one had yet dared to investigate the kitchen too closely. Now a young missionary volunteered to work there himself and Ken felt that as unofficial public health officer, he had the right to go and see for himself. Up to that time with the fear of the 'gang's' reaction, no one had dared to do this. His visit was greeted with considerable resistance and he himself, was horrified at what he saw. The place was smoky from the wood fires and full of steam. The floors were wet so that the cooks had to stand on duck-boards to keep their feet dry. There was filth everywhere and food was being handled with unwashed hands. The young man working there reported that just as we had suspected, food was being taken out of the rations and put aside for the kitchen staff.

Ken really had no authority from anyone to deal with the situation and this was obviously needed before anything else could happen. In the early morning they considered this and came up with the idea of holding camp elections. Each dormitory would elect its own room captain who would form a camp committee ready to share the responsibility for decisions and the consequences of going to the Japanese with requests. The suggestion was met with enthusiasm and electioneering commenced. The man elected to be captain in our own room boasted that in his pre-internment life in Shanghai, he had never walked futher than the distance from the door of his car to the door of his club and he looked like it, florid and overweight. But apparently he had been an athlete in his student days and as the months went by and the weight dropped off so his athletic good looks returned.

One of the committee's first jobs having elected our friend the river pilot as chairman, was to organise the food distribution. This quite apart from the kitchen, had been very arbitrary up till now with considerable variation in the size of helpings and several people going round for a second or third time. A group of respectable senior citizens were approached including the Bishop and another distinguished looking gentleman who wore a monocle, and they sat four at a time in a row at the end of the common room nearest to the kitchen with huge containers of food between them. As we queued past them in four lines, rather like going through the cash-out at a supermarket, they would carefully deposit a small ladle-full of stew in each bowl while we deposited a brass 'tally', a collection of which had been found left over from the days of the tobacco factory. This ensured that no one could get away with a second appearance.

From what they had seen and heard about the kitchen the committee decided that anyone having to work under those conditions should have extra food to compensate and it was decided that kitchen workers from that time should have a ration and a half. Ken then had the backing of authority to do something about the conditions. Those that did not appreciate his efforts walked out and fresh ones took their place.

The Commandant accepted the new arrangements without question and our former representative seemed only too glad to be relieved of his onerous job. We were now able to put in lists of requests and needs. Some we got and others we didn't. As far as medical supplies went we soon learned to ask for twice as much as we needed several months before we were likely to need it. Now and again the Japanese would organise a trip across the river taking with them one of the teachers, engineers or doctors. These were rare treats so lots were drawn for a place in the party. We would watch enviously from our windows as they made their way towards the river and their return from the outside world was greeted like a breath of fresh air.

Other developments from the committee included the setting up of a library. Over a thousand people expecting to be shut up for a considerable period of time had taken in between them, a large number of books. With the new sense of community and security which had sprung up, people now seemed ready to share their precious belongings and the response to the committee's request for books was overwhelming. During the following months I re-read the whole of Dickens and Scott, mostly when Elizabeth was asleep in the afternoon. Finally a tribunal was set up to investigate complaints within the community and Mr. G. was elected chairman of this. They only ever had to try one case but their presence acted as a useful deterrent. Adverse publicity in a closed community is not pleasant to live with.

School for the older children had started almost as soon as we had settled in. The camp had its full quota of teachers drawn from the various mission schools and Universities round the country and lessons were held at one end of the common room while games, hairdressing and general conversation went on at the other end. Now the community spirit spread itself in other directions as well and all sorts of people began to put their talents at the disposal of their fellow internees. Quite apart from the University and school staffs the camp included engineers, carpenters, artists, musicians and linguists of almost every shade. One could sign up for anything from mathematics and chemistry (without a lab.) to almost any language you chose. I even offered in response to a request, to teach harmony but as it meant trying to sing what I was endeavouring to teach, I soon gave up.

One of the best surprises at this time was the emergence of our old friend from Cheloo University, F. S. Drake. He had been incarcerated in Pootung since it opened and had continued to live his quiet, retiring, scholarly life in his own corner. Now he suddenly appeared on the public scene offering to give a series of lectures on Chinese Philosophy and Church History, hardly subjects we thought to have a wide appeal, but they were an immediate success. People of all shades and background poured in in their hundreds captivated by his own enthusiasm for his subjects. At the end of the course on Chinese Philosophy which had included the latest information on oracle bones, the class presented him with a cow's scapula autographed by as many as could get their signatures on to it.

It was not only his lectures which drew the crowds, but having got to know him through them, the Sunday services at which he was preaching were always particularly well attended.

Pootung University continued to thrive up till the end of the war and by then it was estimated that eight hundred people were attending classes on any one day, some of them, of course may have been going to more than one. Many more attended the odd lecture or part-time course.

Alongside this educational explosion, the Arts also began to flourish. A wealth of dramatic and musical talent emerged and productions became more and more ambitious. Some individuals who had never acted in their lives before became stars overnight. The productions included several Shakespeare plays, 'Bitter Sweet', 'Hobson's Choice' and 'The Importance of being Earnest'. The costume designer would draw pictures of the costumes as they should be and then Betty and one or two others would go round the cubicles in the various dormitories begging for loans of anything which might be appropriate. As time went on, refusals to lend became fewer and fewer.

The common room was always packed for these shows which took place on a platform made out of the tables which were normally arranged at intervals across the room. Dreariness, homesickness and the horrors of war on our doorstep were forgotten for these few hours.

CHAPTER 23

THE BAND which had greeted us at the gate on our arrival continued to provide music for dancing on the Saturday evenings on which there was no other form of entertainment. They had played together in Shanghai and the way they played was enough to make the most sedentary jump to their feet. One of their self-appointed tasks was to find out the dates of people's birthdays, having done which they would take up their position outside the victim's cubicle to trumpet and saxophone their way through 'Happy Birthday . . .' This of course, drew the crowds whereupon they played it through again with everyone joining in the singing while the poor recipient of these attentions stood blushingly by.

月光之下

Another almost hitherto unnoticed inmate of the camp now made his appearance in the form of an ex-military bandmaster who offered to turn these jazz wizards into producers of classical music. The leader of the band, an American Jew, had always harboured an ambition to be a classical violinist but for economic reasons had found himself stuck with the sort of music needed in dance halls and hotel lounges. The double bass player, a genial black American, had never learned to use the bow though fortunately he possessed one, and Joe, the bandmaster, taught him how to manage it.

Apart from the band itself there were two piano accordion players and three amateur violin players including my Major friend of Yangchow days. I was lucky enough to be another of them. I had learned to play the violin at school but had not brought my instrument out with me to China. When we arrived in Pootung, one of our Mission colleagues, whose wife had been repatriated, lent me her violin for the duration. Now I had a chance to use it, and out of this motley assembly of individuals and instruments, Joe created his symphony orchestra. Every day he rehearsed us for an hour quite ruthlessly, trying to instill into us some of the discipline he had expected from his army experts. It was an exhilarating experience.

The jazz band, already brilliant musicians in their own right, took to their new classical role like ducks to water and Henry, their leader, was in his element.

Over the next months a concert was put on every few weeks. Sheet music appeared as if by magic. We never ceased to wonder at the things people had brought into camp with them. Most was in the form of piano arrangements needing to be copied out and orchestrated. If no manuscript paper was available then it was drawn out by hand. Much music was written out note by note from memory and this included the Elgar 'Pomp and Circumstance' march much loved by promenaders on the last night of the Proms. Apart from Joe, there were two other fine musicians, one a non-playing American musicologist who did much of the manuscript writing and the other, a nephew of Sir Walford Davies and himself a singer and writer of delightful lyrical music. He was also one of the accordion players and when not performing with the orchestra he would be conducting the camp choir.

Among the music so produced was the Mendlssohn violin concerto when Henry really achieved his life ambition and Schubert's Unfinished symphony. The Japanese are great music lovers and on the night of our concerts, the front row of seats was always reserved for the Commandant and his party. On one of these evenings we finished the programme with a selection of popular tunes put together by Joe. This ended with a flourish of 'Rule Brittania' and the final bars of 'God Save the King', carefully camouflaged by what the violins were doing up and down their strings, but even so, easily recognisable by those with ears to hear. The audience, British first but quickly followed by everyone else, leapt to their feet and the Japanese, not to be left out, leapt to theirs as well and joined in the rapturous applause.

The choir came into its own with a production of Haydn's 'Creation'. A far-sighted member of Shanghai Union Church choir had dashed into the Church at the last moment and grabbed up all the copies she could carry and brought them into camp with her. In this I made my one and only appearance as a soloist in the part of Eve.

All rehearsing was done in the old factory engine room with the huge engine still in place. The Japanese had begun to dismantle it at one point as they saw some use for its solidly British made parts. However one of our skilled engineers, his fingers itching to achieve a bit of war-time sabotage, managed to remove a vital part which he then dropped in the old cooling pond which was the size of a small swimming pool and by now thick with slime and debris. An enraged senior Japanese officer came to the camp furiously demanding to know who had done this dastardly deed. He was given the name of a certain internee and told that this man had been transferred to another camp in the area. What we knew but the officer did not was that this man after his transfer was one of only two to escape from any camp and was by now probably several thousands of miles away in Free China.

Meanwhile the clandestine early morning meetings went on unnoticed even by fellow internees. From the start, Mr. J. had been producing a daily typed news sheet which was pinned up on various notice boards around the camp. In it he published any news which might have filtered into the camp from the outer world and any events of note which had occurred in the camp itself. He alway concluded with a wise-crack of some sort reputedly made by a character he called 'Pootung Pete'. News of the war was, of course, as seen from the Japanese point of view and, as Japan and Russia were not officially at war with each other, we also received endless news of the Russian front with lists of hitherto unheard of and unpronounceable names of Russian villages and towns. Of what was happening in the West we heard nothing.

Ken, still aware of the mistakes of Yangchow, had studiously avoided putting out any advice on public health matters even in humorous form but hearing Pootung Pete's comments on camp life, the scruffy little man himself became a living character, uprooted from his normal life, deprived of freedom, inadequately housed and fed and questioning the reason behind it all. He began to produce cartoon posters of Pete as he observed the goings on of the camp life around him and developed his philosophy. The painting was done with a Chinese brush using a stick of Chinese ink wetted and rubbed in a plate of the kind used by Chinese artists. The best paper for the purpose proved to be that provided by the authorities for a very different purpose but willingly sacrificed for this more positive use. It was rough and absorbent, just the thing for Chinese art. For the next eighteen months Pete appeared every two or three days in a new poster illustrating the follies of human nature which had landed us all in this mess and pointing gently forward to the possibility of change. The posters went up just inside the entrance to the common room and past which everyone passed on his or her way to collect food. As the queue moved slowly by there was plenty of time to look at them. The response was usually a chuckle or a grimace as the message struck a chord. None was ever pulled down or defaced. Only one drew any adverse comment and that was a picture of Margie and Elizabeth fighting over a little wooden cart which someone had made for them and which was well known by sight to the rest of the camp. The caption was 'Gimme and Grab'. People felt it was an unjust smear on the

月光之下

reputations of the camp's mascots. One of the best was of a rather miserable, unshaven face looking at itself in a mirror with the caption, 'Face the Problem'.

It was hard work thinking up new ideas for these posters and in this we were all involved, sometimes willingly but not always. The only place where Ken could spread himself to do his painting was on the table he had made at our end of the cubicle. Normally it hung folded back under the window and when it was up it occupied valuable space, a fact which Betty and I did not always appreciate but looking back it was a small price to pay for what was undoubtedly a major contribution to camp morale.

At some point during this time we thought the camp should have its own coat of arms and motto, so this too Ken devised. In the quarters made by a cross of barbed wire, were various accoutrements of camp life and across the bottom were the words, 'Te vince ut pacem fruaris', which for the non-Latin scholars meant 'Overcome yourself that you may enjoy peace'. This he painted in black paint made from soot and water, on the huge matting screen covering the end window of the common room where it looked very fine.

CHAPTER 24

SOON AFTER we arrived in Pootung some of the men decided to look into the question of fire precautions. As long as matches and cigarettes continued to come into camp and there never seemed to be any shortage, there would be a serious fire risk with the building's wooden floors and pillars and a plentiful supply of draughts. There was a number of hoses rolled up on their reels left over from earlier days and one morning these were unrolled and trailed along the ground round the building. When the water was turned on there were great spurts from holes every few feet along the length of the hose while out of the end came a mere trickle. However the volunteers in the fire brigade persevered and continued to practise regularly with any equipment they could lay their hands on.

Godfrey, meanwhile set about training a First Aid squad. By the end of the war about a hundred people had completed the St. John's ambulance course. Fortunately their services were never seriously needed but with the increasing number of air-raids they might well have been.

The only real fire threat came from a man who had put a hot brick in his bed one winter night hoping for a little warmth. When he went back to his bed to turn in he found the brick smouldering it's way through the floor boards under the bed having burned its way through his bedding and mattress.

One night a Japanese soldier, somewhat the worse for drink, lurched into the single women's dormitory and began to push his way through the curtains of one of the cubicles. A scream from the teenage occupant brought a young tough P.E. teacher to the rescue and with a neat throw the luckless guard found himself on the floor. After that incident regular ju-jitsu clases were held for women usually outside in an alleyway by the side of the building where they could easily be seen by the guards as they wandered by.

Our worst night of terror was caused by a group of mixed nationality teenagers. It happened when I was having a spell in the hospital being treated for a recurrence of the amoebic dysentery which I had picked up while in India on my way out. The treatment in those far off days included rigid bed-rest while one coped uncomfortably with retention enemas. Next to me in the hospital was a slightly mentally defective pregnant girl and beyond her an elderly woman with bronchitis and heart trouble. Across the ward separated from us by screens were three men one of whom was recovering from a coronary thrombosis and also forbidden to get out of bed. Another had a damaged leg so was unable to walk.

I had quite enjoyed lying in bed gazing at the moveable matting screens on which Ken had painted familiar landscapes. My favourite was a small fishing harbour on the east coast of Scotland in which his family and I had spent a particularly happy holiday.

月
光
之
下

There were four trained nurses, all missionaries, who carried the weight of nursing during the day while at night an untrained volunteer would sit up with the patients. On this particular night we had been settled down and a dim light glowed from a table in the corner on which were kept patients' records, jugs of water and other odds and ends. As it was summer each bed was covered by a mosquito net. All was silent apart from the occasional snores from the adjoining men's dormitory.

Suddenly in the middle of the night all hell was let loose. The sound of the barking so peculiar to the Japanese soldier, the stamping of feet and jangling of swords, and the clanging of the roll call bell shattered the peace. Shouting and pushing chairs out of the way, three or four guards stormed into the ward, promptly ordering the woman on duty back to her room, then upsetting the table, scattering bottles and papers everywhere plus the light which then went out leaving us in total darkness. Torches were switched on and the soldiers tramped round the ward shining them on each face in turn. Then as suddenly as they had come they were gone but the noise in the rest of the camp went on for at least another hour.

None of us had any idea of what had happened and I lay on my bed feeling rather desperately responsible for the other patients but powerless to do anything apart from making hopefully calming remarks. No one came near us till the morning.

The windows of the hospital looked out on to the outside staircase leading to the Commandant's office. As soon as it was light, we saw a line of figures tied to each other by a rope, being pushed down the stairs by a group of obviously angry guards. Even from that distance we could see that the boys' faces were swollen beyond recognition and their feet were bare.

When the nurse came on duty we learned what had caused the uproar. Five boys had managed to get out of the camp and had somehow got hold of beer and cigarettes which they were on the point of bringing into the camp when they had been caught by a Japanese Naval landing party who had escorted them back none too gently into camp and demanded their immediate execution. After all this was what we had been warned would happen to anyone caught breaking out of camp.

The camp guards, however refused to do this, saying that the boys were their responsibility and they would decide on their punishment. There was some fierce arguing but eventually the Naval party left having been assured that whatever punishment would be meted out it would be adequate. The boys were then taken to the Commandant's office where their shoes were removed and they were made to stand in a row, their hands tied behind them to a ladder. The guards then proceeded to beat them with rifle butts and baseball bats till morning.

To make matters worse, the office was only separated from one of the women's dormitories by a thin partition so to the yells of the boys as they were beaten were added the screams of hysterical women and the ju-jitsu lass had to perform once more in order to control them and prevent the mothers of two of the boys from breaking into the office. Meanwhile the rest of the camp's inmates were out of their beds being counted and recounted. When morning came the boys were taken off to prison in Shanghai where they were kept in solitary confinement for three months.

There were others who suffered periods of imprisonment in Shanghai gaol but they went off quite gaily knowing all along that this is what would happen if their activities were discovered. They were the creators and controllers of secret radios which throughout the whole two years we were in Pootung, never totally ceased to feed news into the camp. Parts for the radios were smuggled into camp in tins which came in the monthly food parcels. Most of them got through but a few were found and then the whip fell. For crimes like this, the whole camp suffered. Night-time roll calls would be held every night for a week or more and the 'garden' would be closed thus limiting our movements to the narrow roadway round the building and putting the washing troughs out of bounds.

On one such occasion we were totally confined to our rooms for a week and only allowed out to collect food.

The radio news was filtered through the camp by word of mouth, each man knowing only his immediate contact. Ken was one in the receiving line so news travelled fast to our corner but I never knew from whom he received it and certainly never asked.

CHAPTER 25

THE WAR outside us continued to rage and even the news we did get gave us little idea of how things were going. By the end of our first summer in Pootung, the *Conte Verdi*, sitting in the middle of the river between us and the Shanghai bund and clearly visible from our window, was miraculously upright once more, a remarkable feat of Japanese salvage work.

One bright moonlit night we were woken by the drone of a distant plane. It had a different sound from the Japanese planes which flew over from time to time. The sound got nearer and nearer and the vivid lights of tracer bullets appeared in the night sky like fireworks. By this time we were out of our beds with our noses pressed to the window pane. The plane, quite a small one disappeared upstream and we thought it must just be on reconnaisance though even this was exciting enough, but a few moments later it was back again, this time flying low over the water. By now all the local anti-aircraft guns were having a go at it. Then as the drone faded away downstream there was a loud explosion and then silence. It was too dark to see anything clearly though we had our suspicions but the morning light confirmed our thoughts as it showed the *Conte Verdi* back at the botton of the Whangpoo river once more, only its funnels and upper structure showing above the water. A bomb had been neatly dropped down her funnel.

It was hard to suppress our jubilation over this bold and cheeky act. More than the mere sinking of the *Conte Verdi*, it told us that the Americans were well within flying distance when all the Japanese censored news was slanted to make us believe they were on the run. Strangely enough, we had never believed it. Although deeply shaken by the sinking of the *Prince of Wales*, Britain's only hope in the China seas, we never at any time seriously doubted the final outcome of the war but it was to be several months before we heard of the Americans again.

Meanwhile more basically human matters needed our attention as babies began to arrive in the camp. They were a mixture of legitimate and illegitimate but whatever they were they were first and foremost babies. As with the few patients we had who needed operations, the mothers were allowed to go across the river to hospital in Shanghai to have their babies. The only time I managed a trip was to escort one of these young mothers. Sadly I could see nothing of Shanghai through the smoked glass of the ambulance windows.

The problem was what to do with the babies when they and their mothers returned to camp. There was no accommodation for them and a baby waking in the middle of the night in a crowded dormitory is not likely to be popular. One of our own Mission nurses, Jean, who deserved more than a medal for the way in which she cared for people, spent many hours night after night nursing a particularly fractious infant in the dim, damp discomfort of the ladies' toilets. Eventually a small cupboard space at the foot of the camp's water tower was graciously vacated by the Public Works department and after much clearing and cleaning was established as the camp nursery. A variety of cots was created and here the babies were put at night with a rota of women volunteers to sit up with them. Betty and I both took our turns at this and it was an extraordinarily peaceful and moving experience spending the night hours with these tiny witnesses to new life and fresh hope.

For some reason which is now forgotten, the youngest mother to give birth in camp, a seventeen year old Eurasian girl who was unmarried, was not allowed to go to hospital. On January 3rd 1945, a bitterly cold day, she decided to go into labour. As I was the only female among the doctors, she was put into my care in spite of the fact that my experience of delivering babies was still at that time limited to my student days, but with the expert advice and prompting of one of the nurses, Michael was safely helped into the world at 2.30 a.m. in the dark under a pile of blankets. His first yell was greeted by cheer after cheer from the hundreds he had woken up in the surrounding rooms. The only warmth available came from a forbidden electric ring in a corner of the hospital and this we put unblinkingly near the little box in which the new boy lay. This time the Japanese appeared not to notice.

We had remarkably little trouble with the babies. Although their mothers were undernourished in spite of the extras we tried to give them, they managed to feed their babies and enough dried milk came into camp to supplement where necessary. If the war had gone on longer than it did it might have been a different story—as indeed it would for all of us.

Margie and Elizabeth of course, were fascinated by the new arrivals but being three year olds, they very much went their own independent ways. They had no fear of anyone and would often be seen walking through the crowded roadway outside the building, their heads close together and engaged in non-stop chatter. Women and men, would stoop down to speak to them or attempt to pick them up but the small girls seemed to have developed a buffer mechanism against these attentions and apparently unaware of it bulldozed their way happily through.

They provided the four of us with endless entertainment though the noise in the cubicle was often too much for Godfrey who would vanish with his books to the comparative peace of the little hospital office. Ken managed to keep on with his drawing and painting in spite of disturbances.

Each afternoon we would settle down for a period of reading or sleeping and this was the time when Ken did most of his painting and thinking out of the next 'morale' poster. Elizabeth, in her cot, and Betty, on her bed, usually dropped off to sleep. But for Margie there developed a regular ritual. As soon as her mother was asleep with her back to Margie's cot, Margie would begin to remove her clothes. Layer after layer was tugged over her head. She would then start to dismantle her cot. Sheets, pillow, blankets and finally the mattress were heaved over the side and on to the floor. Ken and I looked on, far too fascinated to stop her. Finally off would come her pants and shortly after this a small puddle would appear on the floor beneath her which soon grew into a little stream which wound its way across the slightly sloping floor to a hole near the door where it disappeared. On the floor below us was the hospital and just outside the hospital entrance was a box into which messages for the doctors could be placed. The little stream from Margie's cot, or for that matter from an overflowing canvas wash tub in which the children had their bath, would unerringly find its way into this box which necessitated the fitting of a lid which guided the liquid on to the floor and out of the main door.

月光之下

CHAPTER 26

BY THE START of our second year together we really had begun to feel more like a family and less like a random collection of isolated individuals. Of course in a community of over a thousand people there were bound to be some who never got to know each other or involved themselves in community activities and there were even more who would have no idea of how the gradual transformation had come about. But those of us, and there were many besides ourselves, who had met in small groups to pray, knew that without this such a transformation would have been impossible.

Like any family we continued to have our ups and downs. Good government alone can never provide all the answers, it can only hope to provide the atmosphere in which answers may be found. Betty and I soon realised that if we were to be of any help to anyone else finding it difficult to get on with their neighbours we needed to be sure we were working things out in our own corner. There was no possibility of keeping anything private or pretending things were all right when they weren't. Differences between us, mainly over the children, continued to crop up from time to time but instead of two or three uncomfortable days while one of us, plucked up courage to say 'sorry', we managed gradually to whittle down the time till by the end of the war we reckoned we had it down to under half an hour. On this basis our friendship thrived and continues to thrive to this day. Most of the time we very much enjoyed each other's company.

Sometimes our growing friendship with our neighbours was sorely tried. Our nearest neighbours were a young Eurasian couple. We thought she was beautiful enough but she herself was very conscious of her sallow complexion which was certainly not helped by the conditions under which we were living. She did her best to keep herself looking good and depended for this on her dwindling supply of make-up.

I came back from orchestra practise one summer afternoon to find Betty not sure whether to be overcome by mirth or misery. Margie and Elizabeth were too old by this time to have afternoon rests and this made life complicated because we still wanted ours. Betty had been lying on her bed reading while the two small girls played on the floor. She didn't notice that things had turned unusually quiet till two figures appeared in the doorway of our cubicle. They were covered in powder with their faces painted rather like inaccurate clowns. To Betty's horror she realised that they had escaped into the next cubicle and that neither of the occupants were at home. They had then proceeded to raid Elvie's make-up and had got through all her rouge, two whole sticks of lipstick and most of her talcum powder.

When Elvie returned she was distraught and forgiveness came very hard. Betty, who hated being out of sorts with anyone, went round the camp armed with the small but precious tins of instant coffee which had come in our food parcels and which was usually irresistible but could find no female who was willing or able to swap the coffee for make-up.

Most of the time, fortunately, the children were a great source of delight to our fellow internees and to the Japanese as well. They would often disappear but would usually be found behind somebody's curtains in one of the dormitories. Their favourite refuge was Ivy and Anne's cubicle where the dolls house was kept. Here they would play happily for hours. It could never be too long for Betty and me. One of their delights was 'bomb day' when they would suddenly throw the house and its contents on the floor making suitable air-raid like noises as they did so.

One regular visitor to our corner was a young American whose French wife had not been allowed to join him in camp because France, having capitulated, was no longer an enemy of the Japanese. They had a small girl Charlotte, who was the same age as our two and he would just sit and watch the children as they played. One day he presented me with a brand new shirt, blue and white striped, to be made into a dress for Elizabeth. It is still one of our prized souvenirs.

More than once we had an unexpected visitor in the shape of one of the guards who thrust his hand through our door with a couple of apples in it and then rapidly withdrew. As Ken was walking round the building one day he felt something hard being pressed into his hand and a Japanese voice muttered, 'Baby'. Before he could say 'thank you' the soldier had beaten a hasty retreat but he had left with Ken a beautiful little bracelet made up of figures of the Chinese eight immortals.

Another time we were watching the guards being drilled by their commanding officer. To my dismay, Elizabeth let go of my hand and before I could stop her she had made a bee-line for the commander himself. When she reached him he stooped down, picked her up, put her on his shoulder and went on with the drill.

During the summer a young pleasant-faced sergeant, asked if he could take photographs of the children and promised to let us have copies. We hardly expected him to keep his promise but to our delight he did. Not only that, but when Christmas approached he presented us each with enlargements of the snaps he had taken. He was very upset and apologetic because the quality of the prints was not very good but for us they were as precious as gold, the only record we have of the children at that age.

It was about this time that I discovered that to Elizabeth, the words 'God' and 'Guard' were one and the same thing. Fortunately it was not too late to get her thinking straight on this matter. She and Margie too had their differences at times. After one fierce altercation reconciliation had been achieved which prompted Elizabeth to say, 'If Margie and I can stop fighting then the Japanese and Americans can stop fighting too.'

月光之下

CHAPTER 27

As TIME went on, health became more of a problem. Minor scratches would get infected and ribs began to break more easily. Eventually baseball, a very popular form of entertainment, had to be stopped because of the risk of serious injury. Many of the women became quite seriously anaemic and muscles started to ache making going up and down stairs hard work even for those of us who were still young.

Thanks to a growing appreciation of public health rules, we kept relatively free of infectious diseases though there were the odd cases of malaria and dysentery. When we first arrived in Pootung many men did not possess mosquito nets so Ken rounded up some large ones including our own, and out of these made a collection of small ones, big enough to cover at least the person's head. Hopefully the rest would be covered by a sheet. Now and again in the middle of the night, Ken would get up and do a round of the men's dormitories to check that the most resistant ones were using them. The names of any who failed to do so were posted up on the camp notice board the next day.

With the hot weather came the bed bugs. Most of us had never met these fellow creatures before but we got to know them very intimately over these two years. Every morning we would wake itching, to find the inside of our mosquito net dotted with small, round creatures, reddish in colour after feasting all night on our blood. To squash them meant leaving a smear of blood on the net. They had to be removed by hand and squashed somewhere else. Apart from the irritation they caused with disturbance of sleep, the loss of blood to the victim was not inconsiderable. It could have amounted to at least a litre of blood per night for the whole camp, possibly considerably more.

Ken, in his role of public health officer, organised debugging sessions. As the bugs only responded to direct onslaught, beds were taken outside and hit with a hammer whereupon bugs would emerge from every joint and crack to be stamped on. Our own upholstered settee had to be stripped of any unnecessary covering and its legs stood in tins of water as a deterrent but we never succeeded in eradicating the bugs.

Thanks to the intense cold of winter and the fact that the temperature inside and out was the same, we kept amazingly free of colds and throat infections. Being an enclosed community was helpful in this respect too. People who had suffered year after year with sinus infection in their centrally heated Shanghai apartments, were free of trouble though one lady was heard to remark that she would prefer to keep her sinusitis and her central heating.

In spite of our relative freedom from infection, a delightful nine year old boy who had come with his sister from another camp in the north to join his parents in Pootung, developed meningitis and became alarmingly ill. His parents who were missionaries and people of great faith, had won the respect and affection of the camp as had the children. Everyone now responded in a remarkable way to this crisis. People would walk past the hospital window in silence and voices from the surrounding dormitories were muted. You could almost feel the whole camp praying.

A few days before Basil was taken ill, we had received our one and only consignment of drugs and medical equipment from the American Red Cross. Most of this consisted of blood plasma and we wondered whether this was by way of warning us of possible things to come. But the parcel also contained one lot of tablets which were new to all of us. Their name indicated that they belonged to the newly introduced group of anti-infective drugs which had appeared on the market the year before I qualified. I was therefore the only one to have used them and to know the dose. These of course, could be different and there was nothing on them to indicate how they should be used or for what sort of infection but anything was worth a try so, taking an inspired guess at the dosage, we gave them to Basil. Within two days he began to show signs of improvement and after a few more anxious days, we were sure the battle was won and the sounds of camp life became normal once more. He made a complete recovery. We later tried these same tablets on cases of bacillary dysentery and found them very effective, a fact which interested fellow medicals at the end of the war.

We had our own anxieties with Margie and Elizabeth. At one point during the second winter in Pootung, they developed a flu-like illness and lay coughing and feverish, and, quite unlike them, very listless. Margie lay in her cot with an umbrella over her to keep out the rain which was dripping steadily through the ceiling from the room above. Elizabeth lay on our settee and Betty said later that she had hardly dared to look at her face. However in a couple of days, they were as lively as ever.

The only time I ever seriously doubted my decision to stay with Ken was on one bitter morning when Elizabeth sat on the settee, blue with cold and refusing to move. We had put on all the clothes we could find for her including a dark blue serge jacket and trouser suit which one of the women had made out of an old coat but it seemed impossible to get her warm. It was not all that easy for any of us with the temperature inside the building standing at 16°F.

One of the things we were short of was drinking mugs for the children so Ken made one out of an empty jam tin. He partly removed the lid and bent it back to form a handle. On another bitter day we had made up some milk from powder with boiling water and taken it out to the bagpiper's corner to warm up the children as they played. It never occurred to me just how hot the tin handle would get when the mug was filled with hot milk and the scalding milk, as I dropped it, went all over Elizabeth's foot. By the time we got her back screaming to our room and removed her sock, the skin came away with it leaving a large raw area. We dressed it with gauze soaked in gentian violet; there were no convenient non-adhesive dressings in those days. For the next week we had gentian violet everywhere but her foot eventually healed leaving the tell-tale scar as a permanent reminder of my own carelessness.

月光之下

Another dramatic medical emergency concerned myself. Growing round the edge of the camp were clusters of castor oil bushes and for some reason or other we decided it would be a good idea to produce our own castor oil. I suppose it might have had its uses. To do it meant removing the shell of the beans and then crushing them, so, to make use of the time one evening while listening to one of my colleagues giving a learned talk to the rest of us, I sat in the small medical room in which we were meeting, shelling beans.

All was well but the shells were tough and as I dug in with my thumb nail a splinter of shell broke off and pricked the tip of the thumb just under the nail. Within seconds my thumb was twice its normal size and I began to feel very strange. I slipped out of the meeting and staggered up to our corner on the first floor. The children were sleeping peacefully and Betty, who had gone to bed early, was lying with her back to me. By the time I reached my bed I had no breath to say anything so she went peacefully on with her reading. At last she was alerted by the loud wheezing coming from my chest and was downstairs in a flash to fetch Ken and Godfrey. When they arrived, I had already begun to swell up like a balloon with bright red patches appearing all over my face and body and within minutes was smitten with diarrhoea and vomiting which with the bathroom at the far end of the dormitory did not make things easier. The ricin in the castor oil seed had done its stuff well and I was a textbook picture of anaphylactic shock.

Although it was long before the days of anti-histamines and steroids, we did have adrenalin and as this was injected the asthma gradually eased. I spent the night with my burning feet in a basin of cold water and my thumb held up as high above my sleepy head as it would go to ease the throbbing tightness and was thankful to find myself still alive when day dawned. That was the end of our castor oil dreams.

Without much in the way of drugs to treat our patients, we turned to nature for help. The tiny allotments which people had created out of the rubble of the bombed out village, produced their fair share of weeds. When cuts would not heal the patient was sent out to the garden to eat dandelion leaves. Those with aching limbs or other symptoms of Vitamin B deficiency were made to drink an infusion of plantain seeds and improvement was apparent sometimes after as little as thirty six hours. Results, with the dandelion too were remarkable and left us with an indelible respect for the healing power of Vitamin C.

The low amount of calcium in our diet slowly took its toll. When we first arrived in Pootung a Japanese dentist was coming over once a month from Shanghai. After a while the Commandant called for a volunteer to learn the basics of the job and to eventually take over. A young man who had been a teacher in a Mission school offered to do this and became, along with his assistant, possibly the busiest person in the camp and the dentist's chair was rarely unoccupied. He developed a remarkable skill in fillings and improvised repairs of dentures. Extractions were handled by Godfrey.

There were several occasions on which the Japanese themselves made use of our medical know-how. Several times the doctors were asked to visit soldiers billeted across the road from

75

the camp who needed treatment for minor ailments. One time I was asked to see the Commandant's baby son who had a tummy upset. I was escorted by one of the guards out of the gate and down an alleyway into a small apartment where I was greeted with bows and smiles from his charming wife. I watched fascinated as she unfolded layer after layer of minute kimono-like garments from the little body with the least possible disturbance to him. Advice was difficult as neither the mother nor the soldier who accompanied me could speak English.

CHAPTER 28

AS THE DAYS got darker that last winter, they seemed colder than usual. Food supplies became more erratic and we were more than ever grateful for the small additions from our monthly food parcels which miraculously continued to arrive month by month. They would come over from Shanghai on sampans and a squad of men escorted of course, by guards, would go down to the river to unload them. They all had to be opened and scrutinised by the Japanese before being handed over to their owners. Elizabeth's favourite meal at this time was the often questionable bread spread with lard from the parcels.

The scraps of meat in our bowls became harder and harder to find but for a few delicious days we feasted on the greyhounds from the Shanghai stadium which had to be destroyed as they could no longer be fed. They tasted rather like rabbit. On our worst day we were reduced to half a beetroot per person. It was, as far as I can remember the one and only beetroot we ever saw but that fact did nothing to make it more welcome and one lady was so disgusted that she flung her half beetroot at her neighbour.

We knew that we were not the only ones going without. Our American friend whose wife and child were on their own in the city told us that they were having to queue for hours to buy food as supplies became more and more scarce.

Clothes too presented an increasing problem. Many had already lost valuable clothing in the transfer from camp to camp and what was left was beginning to show signs of wear. Ken and I had one and a half pairs of warm pyjamas which we shared between us. A pair of disintegrating long-johns did duty for the second pair of legs. Needless to say the washing of these garments tended to get postponed. By day we wore everything we could get on. One of the best presents I ever had was a siren suit, bequeathed to me by a doctor who had been repatriated, which could go on top of everything else.

月
光
之
下

Rats became more intimate in the winter months and they too were hard up for food but apparently found some nourishment in the corks of our thermos flasks which were covered only by bamboo wicker work with no cup to protect the cork. Their other favourite food was our Japanese-supplied laundry soap which was little use to us anyway.

One morning as Elizabeth was sitting enthroned on her potty in a corner of our cubicle, a baby rat landed with a bump just at her side. It had apparently come from the ceiling. For the next two hours more baby rats continued to fall on us at intervals. The first one I tried to drown in a bucket of water but it refused to be held under. Neither Betty nor I could bring ourselves to hit them on the head and we finally sent for the ever resourceful garbage disposal team who dealt with them as they arrived in their usual cheerful manner. We were promised that once eleven had fallen down that would be the last of the litter and so it was. Apparently mother rat had been caught by the people upstairs in the elevator leaving the babies unprotected.

None of these things seemed to worry the children unduly. On one particularly cold day as we looked out of our cracked and filthy window to give them something to do, a group of Chinese children went past in the road wearing their padded clothes and hugging themselves against the cold wind. Elizabeth pointed to them and said, 'Look at those poor little kids, they haven't got a lovely home like we have.' Betty used this story many times in later years when counselling couples contemplating marriage on the ingredients necessary for successful home life.

Christmas 1944 found us materially at our lowest. Not only were food and clothes inadequate but we were also experiencing more night air raids and the Japanese seemed to find more excuses for getting us out of bed in the middle of the night for roll call. Letters from home on Red Cross forms which had been few enough, stopped coming altogether, so we felt very cut off from our families. We had all the ingredients to make us feel miserable yet that last Christmas was one of the highlights, not only of our lives, but the lives of many of our fellow internees.

It began for those of us in the choir with rehearsals of the Christmas music from the 'Messiah'. Many happy hours were spent in the engine room while Alec drilled the tenors and basses in their entrances in 'Glory to God', which seemed particularly difficult to achieve. A teenage girl, Joan, who was the daughter of the Salvation Army officer who had been taken and held as hostage by the Japanese while we were still in the Country Club, was to sing the solo, 'Rejoice, rejoice'. As anyone who knows 'The Messiah' will remember this solo is full of glorious and devious runs. Joan had a beautiful voice and sang extremely well but had difficulty in reading music so I was deputed by Joe, the conductor, to teach her the notes. This meant sitting side by side on her bed and laboriously going over the music note by note until she had memorised it. The result was well worth it.

Some days before Christmas, Ken got busy in the common room. On the huge matting screens used to cover the windows after dark, he painted traditional Christmas scenes. The basis of the paint he used was the glutinous residue from the bottom of the pans in which the rice had been cooked. With this he mixed either soot for black, brick dust for red or whitewash scraped off the walls, for white. With these he brought Christmas to life. A jovial Father Christmas appeared out of the top of a chimney pot; carol singers grouped round a lamp-post to sing; there were the wise men on their camels and an old English stage coach in the snow. A considerable length of one side of the room had no windows so on it Ken painted a baronial type fireplace and above it a fine pair of stag's antlers. On one side of the fireplace appeared a warming pan and on the other a handsome bell rope. Below the painted fireplace was painted a fire. It all looked very fine but this was only the beginning. The following day, as if by magic, a wooden mantlepiece made by the carpenters covered the painted one and a day or two later there was a realistic fire created by the camp's scouts out of sticks and red paper. From then on each day saw new additions—paper candles, holly, mistletoe and, of course, dozens of homemade Christmas cards. A hopeful sock was hung up and gradually filled with odds and ends. The whole scene was so realistic that people began to arrange their tables and benches in a semi-circle round it and even to warm their hands at the fire now aglow with the aid of an electric light bulb under the red paper.

While we were in the Country Club, Ken had made a life size Nativity scene. For this we had sacrificed one of our precious bed sheets and on this he had stuck black cloth pasted on to newspaper to make the silhouette out of which the figures of Mary and Joseph, the manger and a lamb appeared. Joseph was holding a lamp in his hand and without any prompting, the electricians fixed up a light bulb behind it. This scene hung over the end wall dominating the whole room.

On the Saturday night before Christmas we performed 'The Messiah'. Everyone came in at the right time and Joan didn't miss a note. The Hallelujah chorus may have been more perfectly sung in other places but never with more enthusiasm.

For days before Christmas, Betty and others had been busy working out tableaux to be presented on Christmas Day. The advantage of tableaux over a play was that people could keep still so only the part visible to the audience needed to be perfect. The costumes having been designed, Betty went round all the rooms begging for loans of clothes or drapes of any kind. One of the Jewish families had owned a silk shop in Shanghai and for some reason had brought exquisite silk nightgowns in with them along with matching silk pants with scalloped edges in beautiful shades of blue, green and pink. These were used effectively to dress the angels, the pants draped over the arm carrying a trumpet, the other arm remaining out of sight.

The two boys taking the part of Roman soldiers undertook to produce their own spears and shields and managed to dig up enough silver foil to cover these and their cotton breastplates. Mary herself was dressed in somebody's rose coloured wool dress with a deep blue curtain falling from her shoulders like a cloak and white veil over her hair. The miracle to us was the readiness with which people dug deep into their valuable possessions to find the best they could contribute and we thought back to the early days of camp life when such a thing would have been unthinkable.

月光之下

On Christmas Eve there was to be a dance. Usually on Saturday nights the dance band built a platform for itself right under the end window in full view of everyone. On this evening however, Henry moved his players to a remote corner of the room leaving Mary and Joseph to look down on the dancers.

Christmas day dawned cold and bleak but there was no doubt which day it was. There was no turkey or Christmas pudding and the only presents were those people had made out of bits and pieces to give each other. Charlotte's mother in Shanghai had sent in a few toys for Margie and Elizabeth including a small cloth bear which was an immediate favourite. Betty had made a nurses outfit for each of the girls which once on were hard to get off. Margie went to bed in hers. I, having thought of it rather late, managed to produce one mitten each for Betty and Margie with the promise of another in due course, knitted out of a long woollen stocking which had lost its mate. Ken had made a butter knife and bread fork for me out of sticks of bamboo, and I made a red tie with white spots out of an old dress. He never wore it but it remains a treasured memory.

The morning service was full and I did my best to make the little collapsible harmonium which a farsighted missionary had brought into camp, sound like a three manual organ. The midday stew was announced on the blackboard outside the kitchen as Braised Beef instead of the more usual S.O.S. (same old stew).

In the evening the tableaux were presented to an audience many of whom until this year, had forgotten or ignored the original Christmas story. The electricians had arranged special lighting effects and others had rigged up curtains. As each tableau was put on a small group of us sang appropriate carols, and as the next one was being set up, everyone sang. At the end of the evening a lady came up to me with tears running down her face and said, 'This is the first time I've known what Christmas was all about.'

CHAPTER 29

THE AFTER GLOW of that Christmas lasted on into 1945. In spite of the cold, the rats and the night time air raids, classes, plays and concerts went on and more unexpected talent revealed itself. The children, though we longed to put more weight on their bodies and colour in their cheeks, played happily with their toys and visited their numerous adopted aunts and uncles. They even called the Japanese 'uncle', one particular favourite being 'Uncle Shumu' though what his real name was or why he came to be called that we never knew. His fraternising with us and the children brought about his early transfer. Certain aspects of the guards' behaviour puzzled them yet in spite of all their barking and pushing they never seemed to see them as a threat. They were just part of, what was to them, normal life.

Over the next months bombing raids by the Americans became more frequent. Often during the night we would wake to hear, not the sound of a small plane but the steady low-pitched hum of the huge B29 bombers high in the sky as they followed the river dropping their bombs on the oil storage tanks and other targets on the way. We always heard them well before the air raid warning sirens started up. The noise of exploding bombs often sounded uncomfortably close. The Japanese had not allowed us to paint a white cross on our roof as we were in the middle of Shanghai's industrial area to which they did not want to draw attention. There were no air raid shelters for us to go to so we lay in our beds feeling very vulnerable. Ken put up our table so that we would at least be protected from shattered glass. For him, it was all an exciting game and while I lay with my head firmly underneath the pillow with Elizabeth at my side, he would be up at the window watching the fireworks.

Eventually we began getting day-time raids as well. The camp by now had its air raid wardens and Godfrey was in charge of the first aid stations set up round the camp. When the raids started he and Ken would rush off to their allotted duty points along with the fire fighters and first aid squads their only protection being enamel wash basins for use as helmets. The rest of us were ordered to stay in our rooms. Our feelings at these times were always a mixture of relief that the Americans were doing something and fear of what might happen. One day as Betty and I with the children were standing cautiously a few feet away from the window watching the explosions and the fires which followed, I glanced down at Elizabeth who was holding my hand. She wasn't even looking at the window but had her eyes fixed on my face. As long as I showed no sign of fear, she would not be afraid. It made me take a new hard look at my own trust in God to take care of us.

Things took a more serious turn when gangs of Chinese were brought to a piece of waste ground opposite our window and a few hundred feet away from the camp wall and started to

月光之下

build a large mound of earth. We guessed long before the actual gun arrived, that this was to be an anti-aircraft gun emplacement. But the Americans were obviously not lacking in good intelligence. The gun had hardly been put in position before they were on to it. One morning the sirens went as the sound of planes got ominously close. We were ordered this time to evacuate our rooms and take shelter on the ground floor. We found ourselves, also for the first time in the middle of one of the men's dormitories and while the small girls entertained the men and F. S. Drake went quietly on with his reading, we listened to the racket outside.

Suddenly there was a collossal explosion which shook the old building and us with it. Plaster and the dust of ages showered down on our heads. After the noise stopped and the sound of planes faded away the all clear went and we trooped back to our rooms.

Everything was smothered in dust and the window, far from complete as it was, had more holes in it, the glass scattered on the floor. Outside across the road, the gun emplacement had been demolished by a direct hit. The Japanese, now realising it was no use pretending anymore, ordered a white cross to be painted on the roof.

Along with all this came Spring and as the first sign of it, Easter. The choir and orchestra had been busy rehearsing Stainer's 'Crucifixion' several copies of which had also come to light. A notice went up outside the kitchen building where all forthcoming events were posted and as I passed by one day I heard a lady say to her friend, 'They've made a mistake. It wasn't Stainer, it was Jesus,' but on Good Friday the common room was packed to hear it. On Easter Sunday there had to be two services to accommodate everyone who wanted to attend. As the hall held five hundred at a time there must have been very few individuals who did not turn up. The spirit we had felt at Christmas was, in spite of minor ups and downs, still very much alive.

The Japanese meanwhile were becoming more and more jittery. The news they allowed us to have and which was published in the daily news sheet, still spoke of Japanese victories but it was clear as we studied the map that this was no more than a victorious retreat as island after island clearly had Americans on them rather than Japanese. Knowing something of their mentality and their likely refusal to surrender we began to wonder what they would do with us when the day of defeat hit them. When they first took us over in Cheloo, we had quite expected them to bayonet the lot of us but they had not done so, but at that time they would have no thought of possible defeat. Now it might be different, but along with these thoughts was the steady reassurance that as God had been with us so far, He would certainly go on being. There were some in the camp who voiced their fears of the future but I think most of us fully expected to survive in spite of all that might point to the contrary.

There were moments during those months when our spirits fell. One was the day an American bomber was shot down. The men on duty outside watched as it fell in flames. The following day one of the great wheels of the plane were pulled by a lorry past the fence for us all to see. Then in the Spring we had heard of the death of Eric Liddell in Weihsien camp in the north. Many of us had known him well and had looked forward to meeting up with him again after the war. We thought of his wife, Flo, and their three children, the youngest of which he had never seen. He was also known of course, by many others as one of our greatest athletes and a large number came to the memorial service we held for him.

Perhaps the worst moment strangely, was on a day in May when the news filtered in sometime round midday that the war in Europe was over. There was subdued cheering in the first moments of elation but this was quickly followed by a bleak sense of abandonment. We could picture the lights going on again all over Britain and family reunions but it only made us more aware of our own blacked-out isolation. We felt very far away and forgotten. I remember thinking rather stupidly, whether anyone would now bother to finish off the war in the Far East.

As the news was not official we had to carry on as though we knew nothing in front of the obviously disturbed Japanese. However, a few days later, the Commandant sent for our representatives and informed them that Germany had surrendered.

The next three months seemed the longest of the whole time of internment. Far from being forgotten, we were very conscious of the hotting up of the war in our part of the world. As the war got hotter, so once more, did the weather. Mosquitoes and bed bugs were at it again. Out came our summer clothes or what was left of them. As we sweated through the summer the backs of dresses disintegrated and had to be cut out so producing an interesting new fashion.

The highlight of camp life that summer was the taking of the Cambridge School certificate exam by eleven teenagers. There was no lack of qualified teachers in every subject and teaching had gone on steadily through the months, space for this having to be shared with all the other classes going on as well as people playing their games of bridge and mahjong.

For four weeks before the exam was due to start, each candidate was fed with vitamin pills which had been carefully kept for this purpose. They had come with the Red Cross medical supplies but there were not enough for more than a few people. The Japanese gave permission for papers to be set by University staff in the various camps who were qualified to do so and the answers were sent back to them for correction.

When the day for the exam actually arrived, curtains were rigged up across the common room and tables arranged at one end for the examinees. The rest of normal day to day activity went on in the other half of the room with everyone talking in whispers, walking on tiptoe and moving their mahjong with the minimum of clatter. It would not be the camp's fault if they did not pass. The exam went on for several days and the camp kept quiet. The examiners passed all except one who was borderline but when, after the war the papers were submitted to the Cambridge Board, he too was assessed to have deserved a pass.

Something happened to Ken and me that summer which greatly encouraged us in our belief that the war would end in the foreseeable future and that we would survive. All through the years of internment we had felt it would be wrong to run any risk of bringing another child into the world under those conditions. While we felt no criticism of those who had, we knew that, quite apart from the risks to the child and the extra responsibility, it could only leave us

月
光
之
下

open again to suspicions of preferential treatment and we did not want to put ourselves in the position of needing special care. Incidentally there were no such things as contraceptives. But suddenly it was as though the lights turned from red to green and we almost sensed that we were being ordered to embark again on raising a family and by the end of the war I was two months pregnant.

One hot July day we were wandering round the building when a plane flew low over our heads, the American star showing clearly on its fuselage. As it passed over the camp, showers of leaflets rained down on us which were pounced on before they even reached the ground. They contained a message from General McArthur, Commander of the American forces in the Pacific. It told us in firm black print that 'We are not far off', and went on to ask us to stay where we were when the end came for our own safety and so that they could easily find us and check that we were all right. The excitement was intense and even though we had to wait a few weeks before we heard any more we knew the end was in sight.

One day we were lined up as usual for roll call but instead of the customary pushing and face-slapping, the guards carried out their job in silence, their swords still jangling at their sides but their faces haggard. All the jaunty authority had gone and they were like pricked balloons. It was clear without anyone telling us that something catastrophic had happened. We had expected a violent backlash with defeat but there seemed to be no spirit left in them for violence.

A day or two later the Commandant informed us that a terrible bomb had been dropped. Many had lost friends or relatives. The Commandant himself had already lost relations in the raids on Tokyo. But still not even the Japanese knew exactly what was going on and we continued to be counted and watched over. One day someone saw a stone being thrown over the wall with a piece of paper tied to it. On the paper were four Chinese characters which read, 'Japan finished. Peace come.'

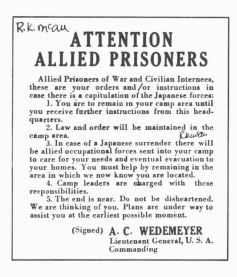

R.K. mcau

ATTENTION ALLIED PRISONERS

Allied Prisoners of War and Civilian Internees, these are your orders and/or instructions in case there is a capitulation of the Japanese forces:

1. You are to remain in your camp area until you receive further instructions from this headquarters.

2. Law and order will be maintained in the camp area.

3. In case of a Japanese surrender there will be allied occupational forces sent into your camp to care for your needs and eventual evacuation to your homes. You must help by remaining in the area in which we now know you are located.

4. Camp leaders are charged with these responsibilities.

5. The end is near. Do not be disheartened. We are thinking of you. Plans are under way to assist you at the earliest possible moment.

(Signed) **A. C. WEDEMEYER**
Lieutenant General, U. S. A.
Commanding

CHAPTER 30

I CAN NEVER be certain to this day which was actually V.J. day. For us it was all uncertainty and waiting. Air raids became fewer and fewer but there was no firm news. One day, however, we were given more firm evidence of help at hand. It arrived in a way which came nearer to killing us than anything we had experienced so far. Betty and I were in the bagpiper's garden with the children when we heard the unmistakable drone of a large plane. Not knowing whose it was or what it might be up to, we picked up the children and made for the building and shelter. Before we reached it, the plane was overhead. Its bomb bay door opened and a platform fell out which promptly tipped sideways and shed its load of huge oil drums which plunged crazily to the ground bouncing as they landed and disorging hundreds of tins, most of which burst scattering their contents of fruit, coffee, tomato puree and almost anything else that can be tinned, over the whole area. The platform, now gently supported by a gaily coloured parachute at each corner, sailed away into the distance.

One man was sitting on his bed when a small tin of tomato puree came hurtling through the roof, landing on the floor by his side missing his head by inches. He commented how ironic it would be to survive the war only to be killed by a tin of tomato puree!

The camp was in an uproar of excitement and delight mixed with alarm at the way the exercise had been carried out. But the first overwhelming instinct was to eat. Ken, true to character, noticed that much of the food had landed on the roof of the factory building across the road. To reach it meant going through the gate. This he did, dodging the guard who quite possibly would not have been sure what to do with him anyway. He somehow scrambled up on to the roof where he sat grabbing up handfuls of peaches, apricots and chocolates, stuffing them in till he literally could hold no more whereupon he was happily sick, leaving himself free to start all over again.

After that first disaster, the Americans quickly changed their ways but it was still essential for us to observe our usual air raid precautions whenever a loaded plane came over. The only difference was that the oil drums with their precious contents now floated down with individual parachutes. Even so, one young mother who happened to be deaf as well as a little slow mentally, was nearly hit as she sheltered with her baby near a wall.

On another day in late July or early August, the camp gate opened to admit an undreamed of sight, an American jeep with four uniformed Americans sitting in it. They got out and introduced themselves as though it was nothing extraordinary for them to be there. One was a doctor, another a welfare officer and another an intelligence officer. They walked freely

月光之下

round the camp questioning our representatives and talking to the Commandant while the guards stood by looking on. Having satisfied themselves that we were as well as could be expected, they vanished again through the gate.

We learned from them that the American authorities were anxious about our likely treatment at the hands of the Japanese when the end came and these men had volunteered to fly in and take a look at us so leaving the Japanese in no doubt that our position was known and their behaviour being watched. They had landed at an airfield near Shanghai and almost before the plane had come to a stop, they had rolled out their jeep before the astonished eyes of the Japanese sentries. Taken completely by surprise, they must have assumed that the war was over and that they had not yet been told so meekly complied with the American request to be taken to the internment camps in the area. Yet another bold group of men to whom we could never adequately say thank you.

A short time after, my memory doesn't tell me just how long, the Commandant summoned our representatives to him and solemnly informed them that Japan had surrendered. He begged us not to treat them too harshly. They were, it seemed, as fearful of us as we had been of them. As the news spread the whole camp gathered at the foot of the steps leading up to the Commandant's office. Then we watched as the Stars and Stripes, together with the Union Jack and the Dutch flag appeared as if by magic at the top of the water tower. The Union Jack belonged to us and had been kept hidden at the bottom of one of our trunks somehow avoiding detection. The other flags had been laboriously and secretly stitched by hand over the preceding days in hopeful anticipation of this moment.

The band, which through the past two years had contributed so much to the morale of the camp played the three national anthems in turn while we stood by swallowing hard but not bothering too much to hold back the tears.

That day, the first American ships sailed up the Whangpoo river followed soon after by the British. For a while the Japanese remained in the camp, a strange and difficult time for them but no one laid a hand on them, and one day they silently filed out under escort, no rifles in their hands or swords at their sides, while we watched in silence. At that moment there seemed no room for thoughts of vengeance. The whole business of the war simply reflected the continuing stupidity of man in which we were all involved and for which we all shared responsibility.

As soon as they had gone, Ken raided the Commandant's office. Others soon followed but he managed to pick up his official seal and the little flat cushion covered with Japanese patterned pink silk before anyone else arrived. In the office was a waste paper basket full of hundreds of torn up Red Cross letters. It was hard to obey General MacArthur's instructions to stay where we were. There was no longer any organisation in the camp though food continued to come in and we had plenty of air-lifted food supplies to get through. One by one people began to drift away, those with homes and businesses in Shanghai going first. The children felt the restlessness around them and were more unsettled than they had been up to that time. Finally we appealed to the American authorities for permission to leave the camp and accept the invitation of an American missionary to stay in his re-opened house in the city. Permission was given and we packed up. On the last morning in Pootung Civil Assembly Centre, we poured out the very last drop of the vitamin oil for the children. The little life-saving bottle was finally empty.

Our luggage was collected and taken off and we said our goodbyes to friends we were unlikely ever to meet up with again with a special farewell to our now dilapidated day-bed which had been such a boon. Then, holding two excited small girls by the hand, we took our first faltering steps towards the gate to the outside world. Our knees were shaking and we felt as though we had just got out of bed after a bad attack of 'flu. The 'next bit of life' had been lived, and was behind us at last.

月光之下

CHAPTER 31

WE WERE WALKING into a world we knew virtually nothing about. Apart from the scraps of news directly relating to the end of the war in our part of the world, we knew nothing at all of what had been going on anywhere else. There had been no Red Cross letters from home for more than a year—they were probably among those torn up and tossed into the Commandant's waste paper basket. We did not even know whether our families had survived or who of our friends might have gone.

Then too, how much had the six years of war altered people's values and attitudes? All this and more went through my mind in the few minutes it took to leave the building and get out on to the road outside. I wondered how much faith had suffered and whether friends we had known and worked with before the war might have given up and stopped bothering to even try to put things right. Knowing the way God works, these were stupid thoughts to have but at least I found myself being asked what I would do supposing it were true?

In the first poster Ken had painted he had depicted us as cave men and women being dragged by Japanese thinly disguised as Roman soldiers, out of our stone age caves, with Pete asking the question, 'Why?' The next one had the answer from a meditative character, 'Because we needed to learn to think'. They had gone on to show Pete looking for and finding a 'Wisdom beyond our own', and the last poster to go up showed Pete, still more ragged but wearing an academic gown and mortar board having just graduated from Pootung University. He now stood at a crossroads deciding which direction he should go in, uphill or down?

We had witnessed what could happen as a collection of 'cave men' individuals developed into a creative community and could see no reason why this should not be possible in any group of people, large or small.

None of us at that moment was fit to plunge straight back into normal life. Godfrey had come off worst and was to spend the next few years in hospital with tuberculosis. We had all lost weight so gradually that we had hardly noticed the changes in each other but we knew we were all paler than we should be. Actually Ken's weight had dropped to eight stone instead of its usual twelve and mine to six stone. He was to continue to have easily cracked ribs for the next several months while I needed treatment for a quite severe anaemia. Betty's dark eyes had sunk too far into her head and her cheekbones were too prominent but the children had done remarkably well. Margie was pale but reasonably plump and her blue eyes still shone. Elizabeth was far too skinny but full of life.

We had a few weeks waiting in the American Mission during which time we bought a few essential items of clothing for the children. The end of the war had caused a slump in the

Chinese dollar and having been issued with a million dollars each by the Chinese Government we found it not as good as it looked. An egg cost 2000 dollars and a loaf of bread 5000. I bought a dress for Elizabeth for a mere 500,000 dollars and a pair of plimsolls for 250,000.

In mid-September we found ourselves in the first party to be repatriated. The *Glen Lyon*, a cargo boat which had carried the first lot of troops to land in Normandy on D-day, had arrived to pick us up. Although it was good to be free, life was to continue to be uncomfortable for some time to come and with very rough weather in the Indian Ocean it was difficult to take full advantage of bacon and eggs or even Corn Flakes and bananas which the children were meeting for the first time. They, with Betty and me, were housed in a crowded cabin on an upper deck but we did have bunks. The women without children and the men had to manage as best they could in the holds of the ship which had been decked over to increase accommodation. Ken slept between the ribs of the hull at the bottom of the hold and could only reach the deck by climbing up a series of vertical ladders, difficult enough in calm weather and when not feeling seasick.

At Columbo we were to be transhipped but the ship provided was not large enough to take us all so here on the dockside in Columbo we said good-bye to the Gale family. Margie and Elizabeth were four years old and have not yet managed to meet since then. They keep hoping. Ken and I had volunteered to wait in Columbo for the next boat and did not regret our decision. Good food, sunshine and swimming for ten days achieved wonders in a short time and when, on boarding the 'Athlone Castle' we were allotted a cabin of our own on a ship carrying 5000 army personnel plus a handful of repatriating P.O.Ws. our freedom suddenly became a reality as we closed the cabin door firmly behind us and were alone for the first time in four years.

Until we could earn money again we would have to learn what it is like to be on the receiving end of charity. We first tasted this when we arrived in Columbo. The Red Cross was on hand once again to come to our rescue and any of us who were reduced to one dress only were given the opportunity to choose one out of a collection of clothes donated by local residents. I found myself near the end of the queue, ahead of us a rack with a variety of dresses hanging on them. I looked along the line and could only see one which appealed to me at all. The rest I would prefer to go without. As each woman reached the rack and started to make her choice, I found unexpectedly vicious feelings rising inside me, until she avoided the one I wanted when I could relax until the next one. With only one to go before me, I was almost desperate and had to fight to control my feelings. If she had taken the one I had my eyes on I could easily have manhandled her. I learned a lot about charity in those few moments. Elizabeth meanwhile, had been whisked out of my arms by a tall girl in Red Cross uniform. Just as I was about to reach the rail they reappeared, Elizabeth, with her fair hair washed and curly, wrapped in a large bath towel and smelling of talcum powder. The girl asked my permission to choose a dress for her as she could not bear to put her old one back on again.

At Suez we stopped again for the benefit of our small group of ex-internees. Here the Red Cross had a major base and a large shed was equipped with everything we would need

88

月光之下

immediately. As we entered the shed we picked up a canvas bag, then followed a blanket each, towels, face washers, toothbrushes and toothpaste, hair brush, underwear and shoes. By the time we reached the exit, our bags were full.

Outside the shed a military band started to play 'The British Grenadiers' and I took refuge behind a door where my eyes which refused to stay dry, would not be noticed though I am sure I was not the only one to feel moved.

Next to the Red Cross base was a German P.O.W. camp. A group of the inmates standing near the wire netting smiled and waved to us and Elizabeth was given a leather dog made by one of them; we named it Tewfik and it became a great favourite.

Ten days or so later, I woke suddenly in the early hours of the morning. Through the slightly open porthole came a smell I had known since my childhood, the smell of the English Channel. I sat up and looking out, saw the unmistakable blinking of a distant lighthouse. Any further sleep was impossible. Exactly at 11 a.m. on November 11th we were anchored in Cowes Roads. Over the intercom came the Remembrance Service from the Cenotaph, the first since the war ended. It is impossible to describe our feelings as we stood in the narrow passage listening to it.

It was early evening before the tide allowed us up Southampton Water. As we approached the docks everyone wanted to be on the top deck on the starboard side. As human mass had replaced ballast in the ship it began to list heavily, forcing the captain to order us to our boat stations. Rather than do this we took it in turns to cross over to the starboard side where we could look out for familiar faces on the dockside. We had been allowed to cable our families to tell them we were on our way but still had no idea who, if anyone, would be there to meet us. Then, as the ship slowly edged her way closer to the flag-bedecked dockside where a military band was playing, we picked out three familiar figures from the waiting crowd, my father, his hair white now instead of the auburn it had been years before, my mother and sister.

The docking process seemed endless but at last we were off down the gangway. The dream I had so often had during camp days of falling into my mother's arms, was about to come true.

POSTSCRIPT

SOON AFTER the war we had news of the Mitsui family with whom we had stayed during our honeymoon in Japan. At the time when Tokyo was being heavily bombed, Mr. Mitsui became ill with pneumonia, too ill to go down to the air-raid shelter. His family chose to stay with him in his bedroom during raids. One morning when, as was their custom, they were together praying and asking for God's guidance, they felt that Mr. Mitsui should be moved immediately to his brother's house several miles away from the city. That night their Tokyo home was destroyed. Takasumi Mitsui and his wife survived to play an important part in post-war reconciliation.

After a few years of hospital treatment in Canada, Betty's home country, Godfrey joined the hospital staff as thoracic surgeon later becoming its Medical Superintendent with a particular concern for Eskimos living in the far north to whom the early European settlers had taken tuberculosis. Sadly he died as this book was being written.

Betty continued to raise a family and look after everyone who came her way becoming amongst other things, a valued counsellor for couples contemplating marriage and doubtless her experience of trying to live peaceably with us came in useful.

Following a period of doubt as to what we should do, Ken and I were helped by a remark made by a friend who said, 'Think of the most needy member of the family and you will find the right plan.' We thought of Elizabeth and her need for a settled home so decided to stay in Britain and try our hand at General Practice. It was the last year during which a doctor could put up a plate at his gate and go into business. When the National Health Service came into being a few months later we had twenty-seven regulars willing to join our list.

Not many years past before Ken, partly forced by the growing number of problems with which we felt inadequate to deal and partly remembering the remarkable healing of Mr. G. in Pootung when Ken had prayed for his wife and daughter, decided to study Psychiatry. He felt God was telling him 'to learn all that man could teach about the mind.'

My own life has continued to be a mixture of family and medicine and what I have learned from life with Ken and our five children has been of the greatest use in the practice of medicine. But the lessons learned through the years of internment, told over and over again as people have asked us to tell them, have not been lost and have kept alive our vision of what can happen through a minority of people determined to find God's way of doing things.

POOTUNG SCHOOL OF·LIFE

PAGES FROM THE PORTFOLIO OF POOTUNG PETE

In 1939 as superintendent of the Mission Hospital in Siaochang, Ken had to travel 400 miles to Tientsin to buy medical supplies.

As the Japanese would not permit these to be carried on the railway, they were packed by friendly Chinese in with the permissible groceries.

At Techow Station a container broke revealing its secret. Japanese soldiers sent a porter to find the owner.

Ken, with Frances making her first trip to their new home, made a rush for the countryside and safely crossed the Grand Canal under the eyes of Japanese sentries.

The journey included being held for questioning by Communist guerillas . . .

. . . and meeting a bandit who let them pass but held up all the following carts.

The night was spent in an inn with Ken in the communal bed. Frances chose a table clear of the floor with its crawling inhabitants.

Having waited for a column of Japanese cavalry to pass by, the welcome silhouette of Siaochang village Japanese fort appeared and with it the thought of comfortable chairs and a cup of tea in their first home together.

MEDICAL SUPPLIES ORDERED IN THE CITY
CHEMISTS — PACKED AS GROCERIES
FORWARDED BY JAPANESE CATERERS

ONE DAY FURTHER SOUTH
PORTERS UNLOADING BROKE
A CONTAINER AND ARE SENT TO FIND THE OWNER

WE RUSH FOR THE COUNTRY — THE NEXT LEG 3 DAYS WALK
PAST JAPANESE SENTRIES ON THE GRAND CANAL —

COMMUNIST GUERILLAS
THEN A BANDIT

ASLEEP ON THE
FAMILY BED IN
A VILLAGE —
AWAITING A
JAPANESE CAVALRY
COLUMN TO PASS

THE SILOUETTE
OF HOME AT
LAST PRAISING
GOD FOR HIS
MERCY

The Mission had stood in the north China village of Siaochang for seventy-five years. Inside the compound were the foreigners' houses, school and church. Outside across 'No Man's land' was the hospital and beyond lay the village.

From the hospital door it was possible to see the Japanese move out from their small fortress, built alongside the mission compound, on punitive missions as they sought to uncover and destroy the Chinese Communist guerillas.

Eric Liddell, the famous Olympic runner had left his teaching job to work as an evangelist in Siaochang. He joined Ken, the only doctor, in going out after a battle to look for any wounded there might be. They used bicycles to travel on unmade roads and across fields.

Eric was ahead when Ken had the sudden thought to get off his bike. As he did so, a hail of machine gun bullets passed between him and Eric. Neither was hit.

As often happened, they were taken off to the guerilla headquarters but this time, instead of being interrogated, they were welcomed for their help and the medical supplies they had brought.

Chinese wounded arrived at the hospital by a variety of means. One man, Lee, was brought in, with his head partially severed from his body, on a springless mule cart.

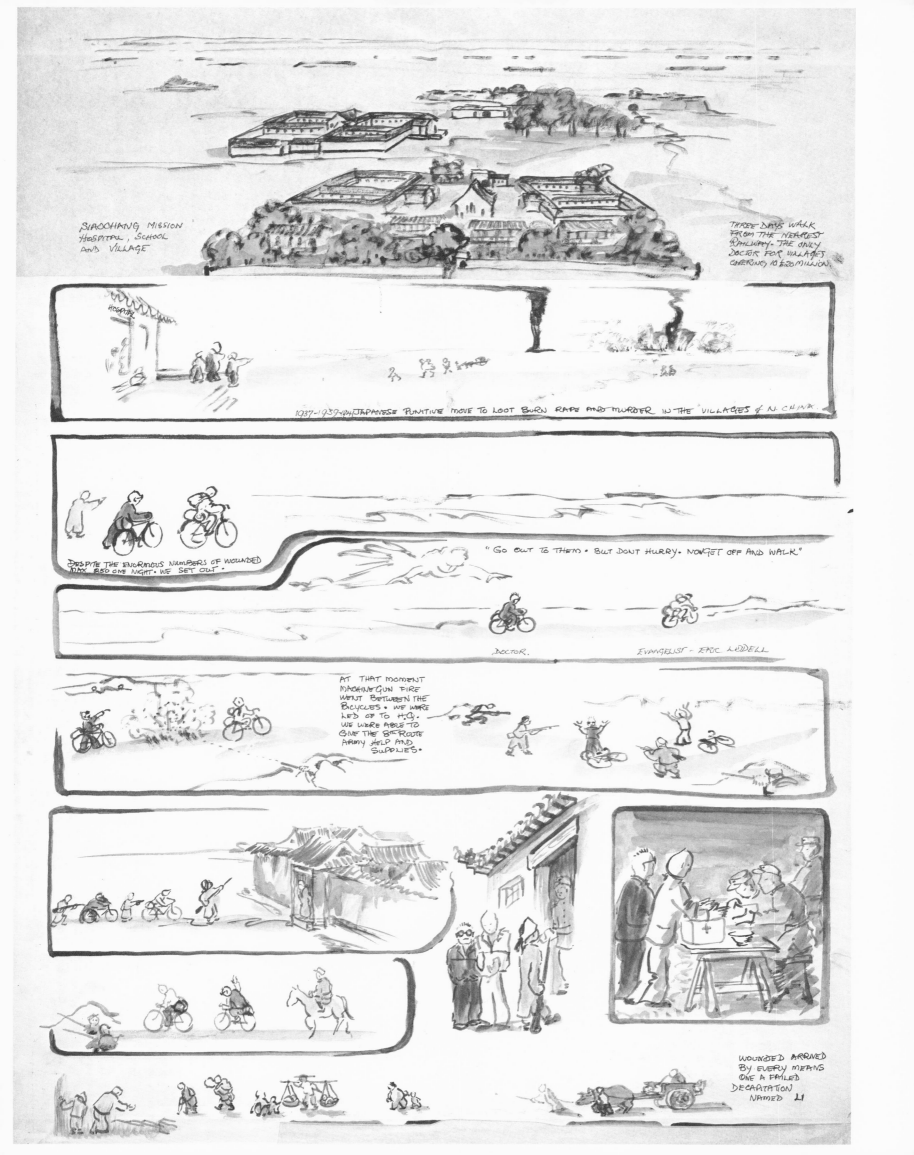

The Chinese Eighth Route army moved in concentric circles with officers and stores in the middle and furthest out, youths with pistols. Only a few officers wore uniforms so the soldiers were difficult to identify. Depending on their information they could either close in to engulf a Japanese unit or open out to let it pass through.

Lee, press-ganged on his way home to join the guerillas, found himself with his unit who had been hiding in a bunker, surrounded by Japanese.

They were all lined up to be executed after digging their own grave but Lee, at the end of the line refused to kneel. The Japanese took an only partially successful swipe at his neck.

The local villagers found Lee still alive and hid him behind an idol in the nearby temple sending a message about him to the mission hospital.

Eric Liddell went off in the mission cart to fetch him. After recovering, Lee took refuge in Ken's house where he did odd jobs, painted beautiful pictures and acted as language teacher.

When Siaochang was evacuated Lee travelled as one of the servants with the departing missionaries, and escaped undetected by Chinese Communists or Japanese whom he feared equally.

A group of schoolchildren needed to be taken forty miles across country to their secondary school in a town on the railway. The parents had made three attempts but were turned back first by floods, then by bandits and finally by a battle.

A deputation was sent to ask the 'big nose' doctor at the hospital to undertake the task. Foreigners stood a better chance of getting through.

As Ken could use the journey to replenish his ever dwindling drug supply, he agreed, little knowing what lay ahead.

First a long walk through the fields . . .

. . . then flood water and the mule cart had to be abandoned and baggage carried.

As they crossed the water in boats tied together, firing broke out from the two villages on either side.

Arrived safely on the far side they made quickly for the next village.

Darkness had fallen when they arrived. Every house and the inn were shut up.

Ken put the children in a pig-stye and slept himself at the entrance.

He heard a cock crow and got the children moving.

OUR JUNIOR SCHOOL GRADUATES WITH SOME
PARENTS WERE TO TRAVEL THREE DAYS TO THEIR
MIDDLE SCHOOL, BUT WERE TURNED BACK BY
FLOODS — THEN SOLDIERS — THE THIRD TIME BY BATTLE.
FINALLY THEY ASKED "BIG NOSE" THE SURGEON
FROM SCOTLAND.   WHO IN SOME IGNORANCE
BUT RELYING ON GOD'S GUIDANCE SET OUT
BY CART THROUGH FLOODS VILLAGES AND
FLOODS AGAIN.   AT A SEEMINGLY DESERTED
VILLAGE FOUND FERRY BOATS, TYING THEM
TOGETHER HE POLED THEM ACROSS. SUDDENLY —

THE JAPANESE HAD BEEN HIDING ON THE WEST BANK
THE CHINESE HIDING ON THE EAST — OUR ROUTE

IN THE MIDDLE OF THE BATTLE WE CONTINUED
FINDING OURSELVES URGED BY A CHINESE ARMY TO HURRY TO A VILLAGE
FOR NIGHT WAS FALLING QUICKLY   AND FIGHTING WOULD STOP.
WE SLEPT IN A PIG STY   AND PROMISED TO SET OFF AT COCK CROW
                              WE SCRAMBLED, TUMBLED, & CARRIED THEM
                              THROUGH THE DARK FOR AN ENDLESS FIVE HOURS
OR SO.   WHY DID THE COCK CROW SO EARLY — — —
                              — WAIT TILL THE END —

Hours later the sun rose and they arrived exhausted at a village where it was market day.

At the Grand Canal every child's bundle was thoroughly searched by Japanese soldiers.

This was repeated at the city gates on the far side of the Canal.

The American mission with its school and hospital was a welcome sight.

Ken having collected his medical supplies set off for home.

Bandits in the middle of the flood water. Thanks to the presence of the big-nosed foreigner, the ferry boats were allowed to proceed unmolested.

Arriving at the village where he had heard the cock crow, Ken found it burnt out and deserted apart from a few old women and babies. Shortly after he and the schoolchildren had left, the Japanese had arrived, confiscated all the carts, absconded the men and boys before setting fire to the village.

Ken gave thanks for the miracle cock and went on his way contemplating the failure of violence and hate to achieve a change of heart.

WHEN AT LAST THE SUN ROSE WE LAY DOWN EXHAUSTED
FURTHER ON A VILLAGE REFUSED US ADMISSION AFTER ANOTHER
HOUR WE FOUND A VILLAGE WHOSE TURN IT WAS TO HOLD A MARKET
- EVERY FIFTH DAY - FED, RESTED WE WALKED AGAIN - - - -
MORE FLOODS, SOME CHILDREN HAD TO BE CARRIED ACROSS

AT THE GRAND CANAL, BIGNOSE WAS
FORCED TO OPEN EVERY CHILDS BUNDLE.
THIS REPEATED AT THE CITY GATES AND
AGAIN ON EXIT TO REACH THE SCHOOL.

THIS SCHOOL, HOSPITAL, EVANGELISTIC CENTER IN ITS OWN
WALLS WAS A WELCOME SIGHT WITH GREAT RELIEF THE
CHILDREN WERE TAKEN TO THEIR DORMITORIES. BIGNOSE
WASTED NO TIME — PICKED UP MEDICAL SUPPLIES AND SET OF WEST
GRAND CANAL — RECOGNISED FOR ONCE! — THEN THE FLOOD
WATERS AGAIN — BUT THIS TIME

BANDITS !
AFTER MANY THREATS
THEY LET US GO, FOR
SOME FOOD ONLY TO
"SAVE FACE" IN THE
PRESENCE OF BIGNOSE
WHO PRETENDED HE
COULDNT UNDERSTAND.

BUT THE VILLAGE OF THE COCK CROW WAS A DESERTED
BURNT OUT SHELL. THE JAPANESE ADVANCED IN THE DARK
AND A FEW MOMENTS AFTER WE HAD LEFT KILLED ALL BUT
THE AGED AND A FEW BABIES

SADLY SET OFF FOR BASE
WHY IS MAN CRUEL TO MAN
IT NEVER ACHIEVES A CHANGE OF HEART.
ONLY LOVE CAN.

Jinan, North China, 1941. Cheloo University busy and happy in the December sunshine.

December 8th, morning chapel, taken for the first time by a student, had just ended.

In the University hospital, out-patients were arriving.

Suddenly one of the foreign staff found his office invaded. War had broken out between Japan and the western Allies.

Within twenty-four hours all Chinese, staff and students had been turned out of the University.

Friends and work had gone. What would the Japanese do with us?

From the hospital, laboratories and libraries, all valuable equipment was looted.

Food soon became the prime need so everyone began to dig.

Coal was available from the University cellars after dark.

Pete and his friends found plenty of time to study.

He found that he could work off his feelings best on jobs that helped the community.

They went to the Corporal now in charge of the University but after keeping them standing for two hours, he turned down all their requests.

Occasional shopping trips were permitted under escort.

The Corporal much enjoyed his new authority.

With time to spare, Pete mastered the Chinese bow and arrow.

He broke into 'sealed' buildings to rescue valuables.

One day the Corporal announced that he had repatriation tickets for everyone.

August '42, local Japanese civilians were told they could 'buy' all Pete's household goods and furniture.

To avoid it being confiscated Pete secretly handed over money to students in the city hoping it might be used to finance their travel to Free China and his, if he could manage to escape.

The escape plan was rejected as the Chinese thought it too dangerous for Pete and his family.

The idea had been that Pete, his wife and baby, would be escorted by students through the mountains, travelling by night and hiding by day.

The day for repatriation arrived but this examination of his luggage damped Pete's excitement.

Thirty-six hours on the train with the temperature at 108°F meant that food went bad and some had food poisoning.

Packed like sardines, they crossed the mighty Yangtse river.

Nanking station platform was Pete's bed for the night.

Pete arrived in Shanghai only to find the repatriation ship already full. So sailed the *Swindle Maru*.

Abandoned in Shanghai, the Japanese authorities issued him with an armband and left him to roam.

He saw door keepers, dead bodies in the gutters, bribery.

Eastern indulgence and Western indifference.

Pete made many friends in the city but found it wiser to visit them after dark.

For six months through the winter, three hundred, from all over China, were housed in a Club. Ninety slept in the bowling alley.

There were other inhabitants of the Club.

As soon as camps could be got ready, Pete and his companions were to be interned more securely 'for their own safety'.

March 8th '43, labelled and numbered, they were ready to march off.

A large river steamer awaited them. They felt like heroes as crowds waved them off.

Destination unknown, Pete felt less bold as Shanghai's skyline faded into the distance.

After twenty-four hours, Chinkiang came in sight and a fleet of open barges.

They had been offered one meal of almost pure curry.

After being counted off on to the barges . . .

. . . they spent three hours travelling up the Grand Canal in pouring rain. They felt cold, hungry and depressed.

On the banks of the Canal, old buildings looked back over hundreds of years of freedom.

The barges finally tied up at the ancient city of Yangchow where Marco Polo was governor in 1260.

In single file and heavily laden, Pete and his friends plodded through the city streets.

At last a heavy gate swung shut behind them.

In the grounds of what had been a school, Pete opened his baggage to find bedding and clothes replaced by bricks.

Bugs!

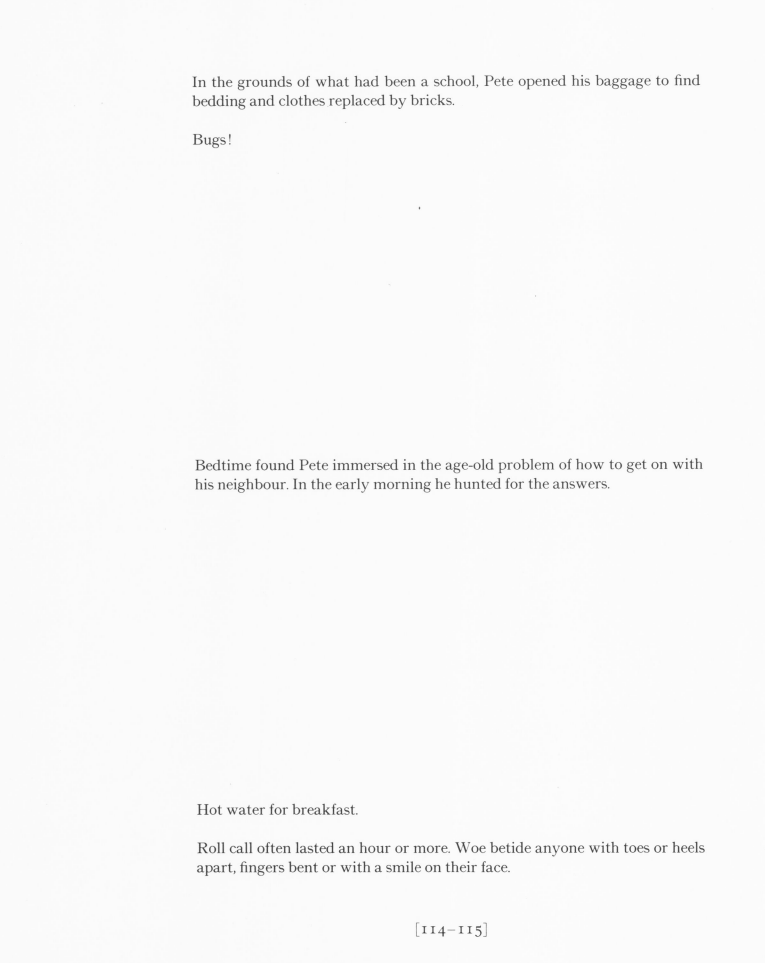

Bedtime found Pete immersed in the age-old problem of how to get on with his neighbour. In the early morning he hunted for the answers.

Hot water for breakfast.

Roll call often lasted an hour or more. Woe betide anyone with toes or heels apart, fingers bent or with a smile on their face.

House work was primitive.

Water for all purposes was carried from the filthy Canal.

It was wiser to let it settle before use.

Once a week a bucket of warm water was available for bathing.

To begin with there was soap for laundry.

Sewage went through a hole in the wall where farmers contracted to buy it.

'The art of our necessities makes vile things seem precious.'—*Julius Caesar*

They passed the time by toasting mouldy bread.

Three days without fuel meant no water could be boiled for drinking.

Food supplies, when not interrupted by guerilla action, averaged 1200 calories a day.

Cooking was done on Chinese style stoves.

Same old stew! Hunger pains passed as Pete tightened his belt.

Emergency operation to remove an appendix with improvised materials helped to restore confidence badly shaken by loss of freedom.

Inoculations against typhoid and cholera were compulsory.

Patients were given a souvenir certificate.

The weekly search for concealed food which might attract flies or rats.

Suspects! A visit to the dentist was the only excuse to get out of camp. How do you prove you've got toothache?

Individualistic agitators about almost anything caused division and unhappiness.

Even good ideas could cause war. They needed milk for the children but how to get it?

Pete wondered if human nature could ever be different.

Rare food parcels provided the only currency. Some would barter everything for cigarettes.

Pete's only contacts with the outside world were few and far between but ...

... 'Stone walls do not a prison make!'

In digging a garbage pit Pete was excited to find a piece of Sung pottery.

From what he had seen Pete could picture some of the beauty outside the walls of the camp. At night he heard ancient temple bells ringing.

Dandelions and spiders caused official wrath.

Pete sometimes gave lectures on life and how to live it. Most people did not want to be told.

Meanwhile camp leaders stored up coal and rice against lean days which became more and more frequent.

A notice in Japanese went up and hung ignored for several days.

When interpreted Pete found he had to pack up everything in twenty-four hours ready for departure.

With luggage and bedding gone he had to sleep on the floor for three nights.

By day they practised lining up and marching. By night they listened to guerilla fighting outside.

Finally the gate was opened and they marched out in silence.

Over a wooden bridge to waiting barges, this time with roofs but no rain.

Pete was still a prisoner but free to enjoy beauty.

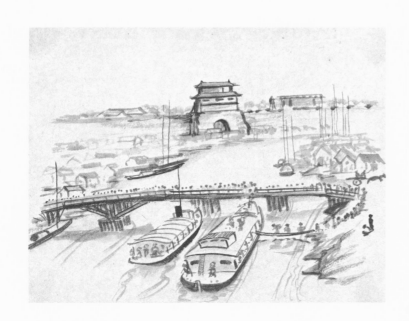

Landed at Chinkiang they were marched to the station.

On the train they were locked in for a night journey—destination uncertain.

Blinds down and no peeping or else...

With great relief Pete found himself back in Shanghai.

Most families went to family camps but Pete was sent with his family across the river to Pootung. In the middle of the river lay the scuttled Conte Verdi.

He arrived at a condemned tobacco warehouse in a derelict factory area.

To the nine hundred men already there the arrival of the party which included two hundred women caused a sensation.

The camp band gave them an overwhelming welcome.

Sixteen rooms for twelve hundred people.

Till beds arrived, Pete shared the floor with rats.

Taps were a novelty . . .

. . . and so were chains.

Pete found there were classes he could attend. Some subjects were popular . . .

. . . and some were not.

Bed bugs made sleep difficult.

Keep fit! Fit for what?

The wall of patience.

Confined to room for one month, crime unknown.

A rope to tie you with, a notebook for your number etc. The guards' daily routine.

Imaginary view of the camp with sundry factories used as military dumps and barracks. The Poo river and Shanghai beyond.

Punishments for minor offences.

These boys got out at night to get cigarettes. They were caught, beaten all night and sent for solitary confinement in a Shanghai gaol.

This man had his hands behind him during roll-call.

Japanese guards worked off their feelings in these ferocious bouts.

Winter and anything that could be worn was put on.

Home-made electric hot plates came into use but only with someone on guard.

Digging for a garden in the remains of the bombed village surrounding the building.

Existing mosquito nets were cut up to provide some cover for all.

Voluntary drain cleaners, the most cheerful people in camp.

In the Yangchow camp Pete had introduced health posters but orders were resented and posters torn down.

He had portrayed basic facts . . .

. . . and even tried to be funny but his advice was still ignored.

New proverbs were invented . . .

. . . but with little effect.

Now in Pootung, Pete tried to think out with his friends posters which would meet the real needs.

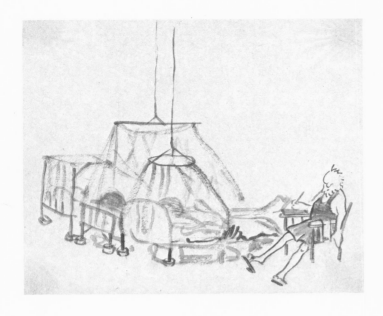

There were deaths . . .

. . . births . . .

. . . and marriages.

When permission had been obtained, surgical emergencies went by sanpan to Shanghai.

Over one hundred people passed St. John's ambulance exams.

Pootung Pete appears for another souvenir certificate.

Food figures were recorded and analysed.

Made to protect the two smallest members of the camp from the attention of adoring adults.

POOTUNG CAC No

VACCINATION
TYPHOID
PARA T. A
B
CHOLERA
NAME

JUNE
1944

A shattering moment when a dying man asked the doctor to pray for his absent family from whom he had felt very divided. He was suddenly healed.

'I am quite well. What can I do to help?'

A daily news sheet was produced.

Gossip became less destructive and . . .

. . . confidence in the doctors grew.

Access to the Japanese authorities became easier but . . .

. . . night patrols carried out by the guards were as disturbing as ever.

A new leadership group began to meet in secret under the staircase.

Food parcels from Shanghai via the Red Cross began to arrive regularly each month. For Pete and many of his companions these were a gift from a Chinese friend.

Working together unloading parcels brought people together.

Each parcel was examined but jam tins often held parts for clandestine radio sets.

Conditions encouraged the collapse of moral standards. A gang of self-styled police bullied the camp. Rations were irregular and theft was rife.

Pete realised that trying to be good on his own was not enough. From then on the nucleus of determined people decided to meet regularly in the early morning to ask God what to do.

First result—a disciplined police force of picked men appeared in the camp and the atmosphere changed overnight.

Talent began to appear everywhere and was organised into weekly entertainment. This was a performance of Haydn's *Creation* in the communal room.

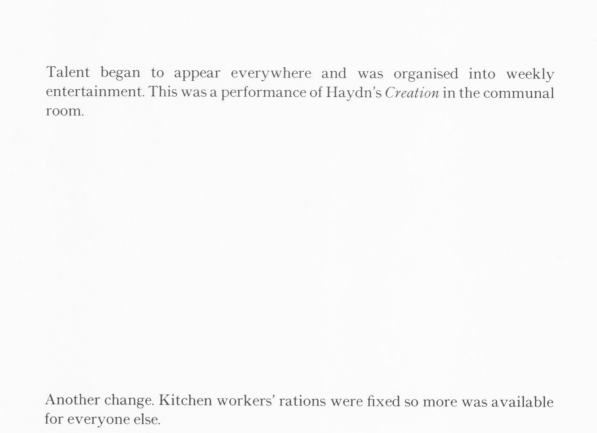

Another change. Kitchen workers' rations were fixed so more was available for everyone else.

Food was carried to the common room.

A picked and trusted team ladled it out.

A stove was built for reheating rations or creating new dishes from anything available. The only warm spot in winter.

Out of junk found on the premises a hot water system was made allowing a pint of boiling water per head.

November '44 the first Allied raider to appear neatly sank the salvaged *Conte Verdi*. Air raids increased in frequency until at the end they were almost continuous.

Raids brought more damage to already broken windows which were held together with bits of paper.

Scramble for safety.

With the coming of winter Pete devised his winter shelter. The temperature dropped to 16°F inside as well as outside.

Signs of intensive preparation appeared apparently for the defence of Shanghai.

Local Chinese were brought in to build tank traps and gun emplacements within a few hundred yards of the camp building.

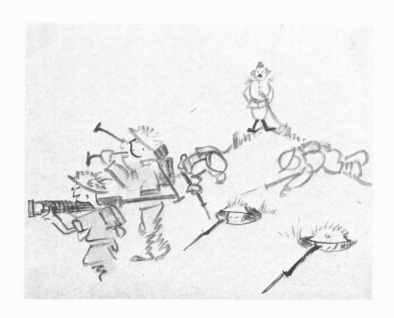

The nearest bomb landed in soft mud a hundred yards away.

Pete enjoyed a grandstand view of the softening up of Shanghai while the guards kept under cover.

August '45, a passing Chinese threw a stone over the wall. Tied to it was a piece of paper on which were four characters—'Japan conquered. Peace come.'

A few days later American planes dropped leaflets with orders to stay where we were when the end came.

Communist guerillas appeared in Shanghai streets . . .

. . . and Nationalist soldiers flew in. They had fought the Japanese for eight years.

The river filled with an Allied task force. The guards walked off unmolested to their own internment.

Pete tottered out of the gate as though he had risen from a sick bed. The sky was blue and the Allied flags fluttered from the roof tops.

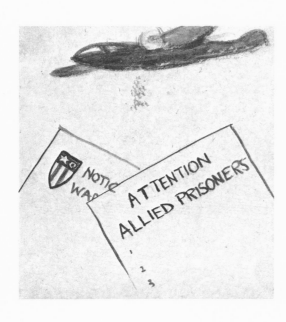

Free to cross the river.

One small four-year-old was terrified by waving branches over her head—the first she had seen. 'It's all green.'

Pete's family sat on proper chairs at a proper table.

A real British ship arrived to take him home...

... but berths were in the hold and the weather was very rough all the way to Columbo.

After that, first class accommodation on a requisitioned passenger liner with a stop at Suez for clothes and other basic necessities.

The English Channel at last.

All five thousand troops and repatriates wanted to be on deck as the ship approached the docks. Flags flew, a band played and long-separated families waved to each other. Pete was home.

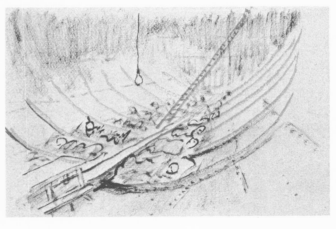

Christmas scenes painted on the large matting screens which were used to black out the windows in the Common Room. (The round stamp in the corner of some of these was the official stamp of the Commandant appropriated by Ken at the end of the war.)

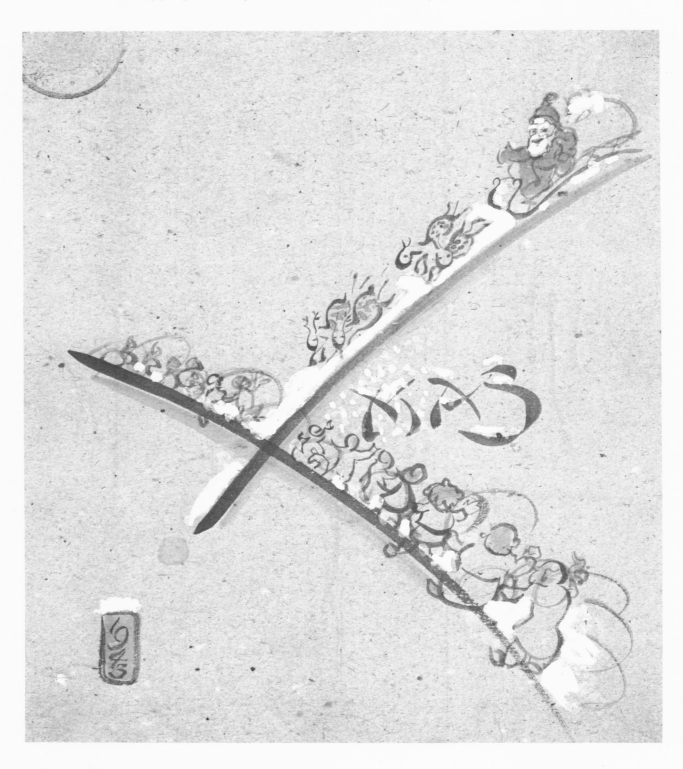

Painted with brick dust, coal dust, and whitewash mixed with the glutinous residue from the rice cooking, this baronial fireplace became the hearth around which people gathered in the evenings.

Pages 155–56. On the moveable matting screens separating the male and female patients in the eight-bedded hospital ward, Ken painted nostalgic scenes of home.

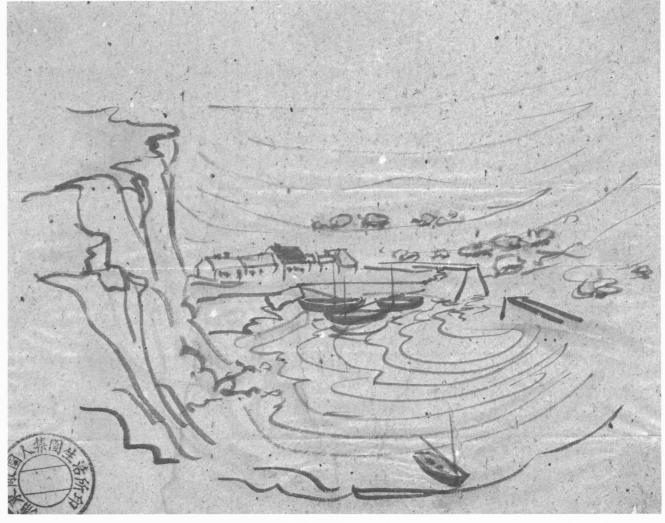

WHY WERE WE DRAGGED OUT OF OUR COMFORTABLE CAVES

 BECAUSE WE NEEDED TO LEARN TO THINK

LAUNDRY LINES

POOTUNG PETE ASKS IS CIVILISATION ONLY SHIRT DEEP

 IS HUMAN NATURE STILL THE SAME ?

AM I
No 1 SHOVING ?

WATER QUEUE

 No 2 BRIBERY ?

 No.3 AM I GREEDY?

MEAL Q

HEAVEN

POOTUNG CAMP

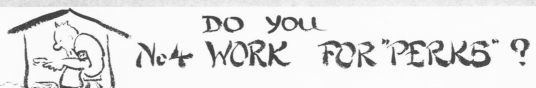

DO YOU
№4 WORK FOR "PERKS"?

KITCHEN SQUADS HOPE FOR EXTRA RATIONS

 No5 GOSSIP

 № 6 GIMMIE & GRAB ?

 NO.7 AM I SELFCENTERED?

CAMP WATER TOWER

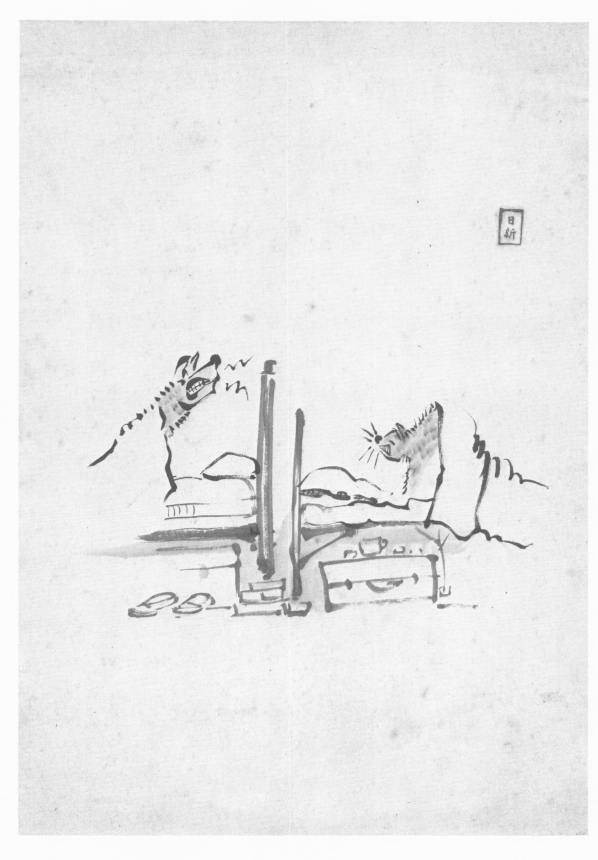

THAT AWFUL FELLOW IN THE OTHER BED

THIS NEW DISEASE
A POOTUNG PHRASE
—"WE ARE NOT SPEAKING
NOWADAYS"

A FELLOW FEELING MAKES US WONDEROUS KIND

 "LOVE'S" BLIND
BUT THE
NEIGHBOURS
AIN'T

 SAVE YOUR BREATH
TO COOL YOUR PORRIDGE

ARE YOUR THOUGHTS WORTH WORDS ?

 ARE MY THOUGHTS WORTH WRITING DOWN

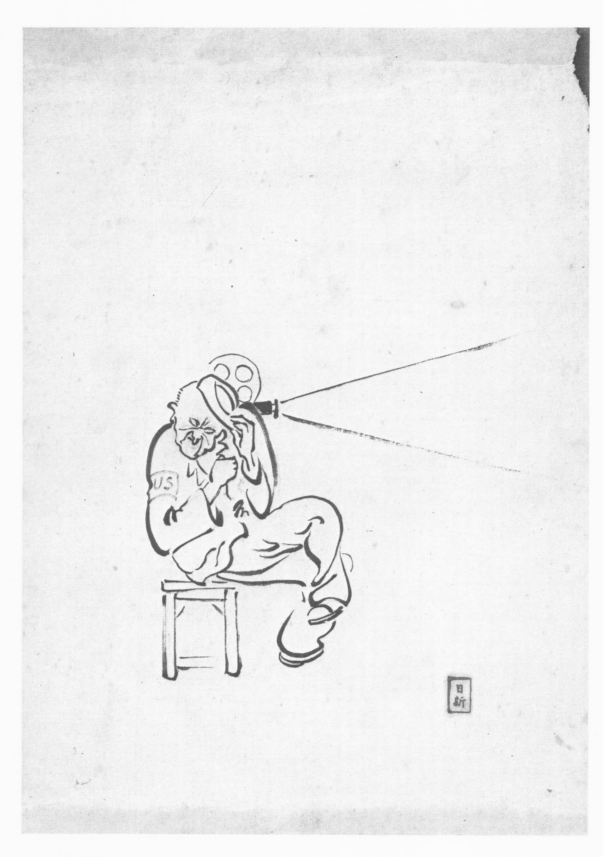

 COULD MY THOUGHTS BE THROWN ON A SCREEN

TOO BUSY TO THINK

 IS THOUGHT FOR FOOD MY ONLY FOOD FOR THOUGHT

WHAT AM I PRESERVING MY BRAIN FOR

ALCOHOL SMUGGLED IN BY GUARDS

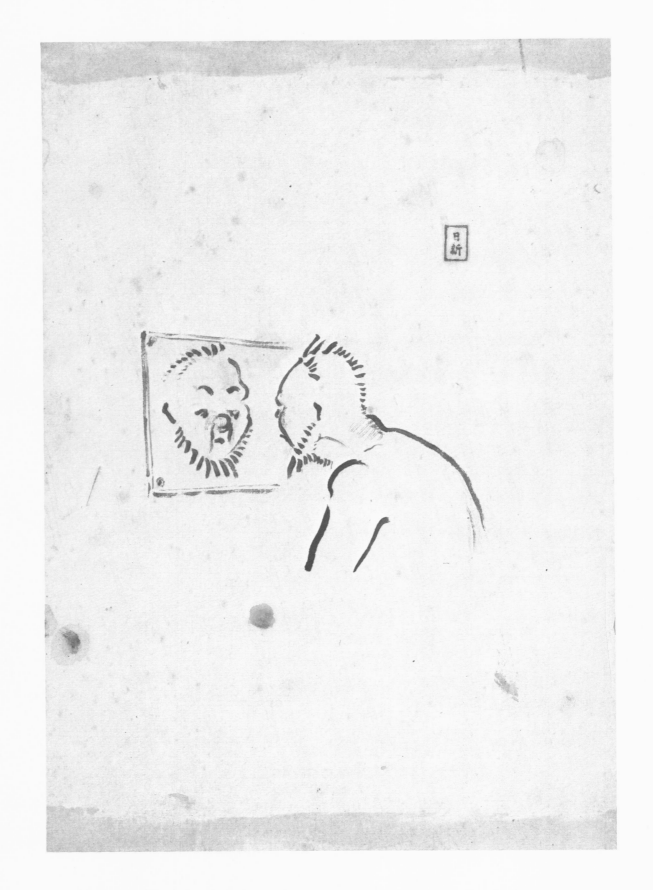

 FACE THE PROBLEM

 WHATS WRONG WITH ME ?

 CAN HUMAN NATURE BE CHANGED
?

ONLY GOD
CAN CHANGE HUMAN NATURE

WHEN MAN LISTENS
GOD SPEAKS
WHEN GOD SPEAKS
MEN ARE CHANGED

QUIET AT LAST

85 TO A ROOM   SILENCE AT NIGHT ONLY

 LISTEN TO A WISDOM BEYOND MY OWN

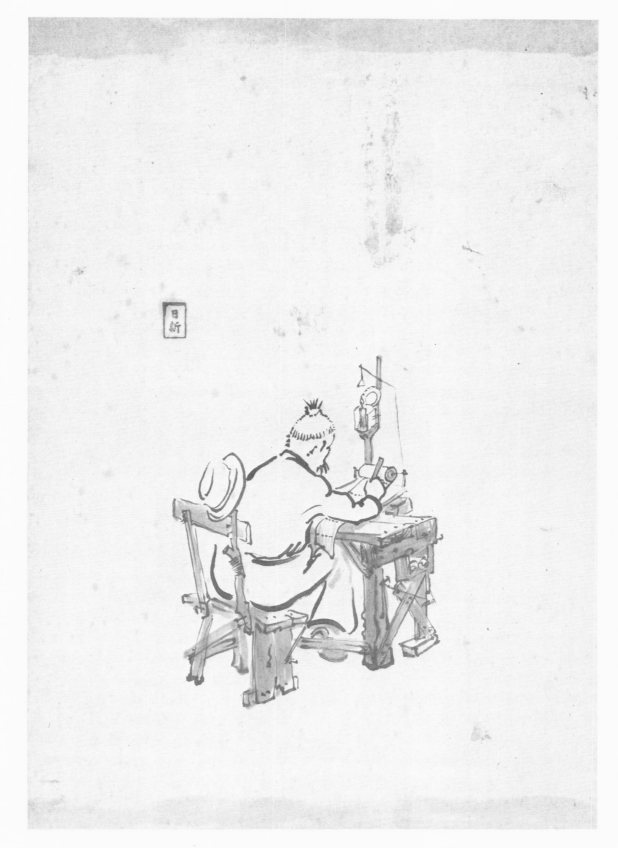

 WRITE DOWN YOUR THOUGHTS

THE FUTURE

ARE WE AFRAID
OF THE FUTURE ?

GOD CAN DIRECT
    YOUR FUTURE

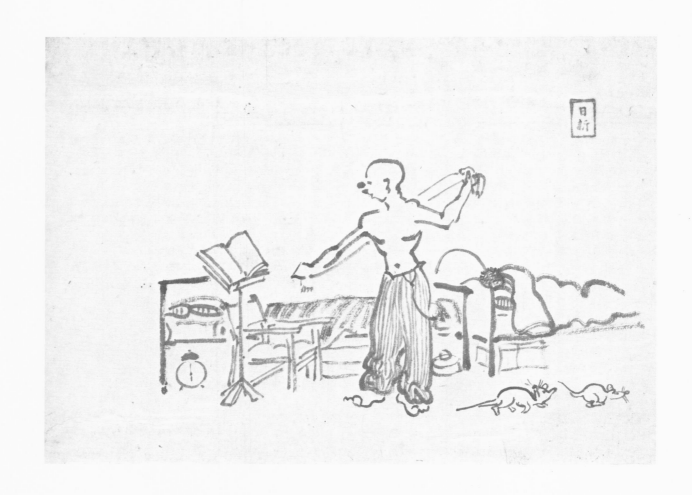

 TE VINCE ..
MAKE YOURSELF FIT
FOR THE FUTURE

UT PACE FRUARIS

V.J. GRADUATION DAY